Praise for *The Sales Leader They Need*

"Whether you're an experienced sales leader or just starting out, this book is a must-read for those looking for a playbook to win the hearts and minds of their team while driving the revenue success that comes with it."

RYAN BARRETTO, president of Sprout Social

"If you're a sales leader struggling to figure out how to invest your limited time and attention in the face of overwhelming pressure to deliver revenue, *The Sales Leader They Need* is for you! Here David Priemer provides a powerful, research-backed dose of clarity into the skills, tactics, and behaviors that will have the biggest impact on your bottom line."

DORIE CLARK, *Wall Street Journal*–bestselling author of *The Long Game* and executive education faculty at Columbia Business School

"Packed with stories, strategies, and science, *The Sales Leader They Need* is a highly researched and well-written book that should be on the shelf of any sales leader looking to coach, inspire, and hold their team accountable for the revenue and personal growth they're after."

MARK ROBERGE, founder at Stage 2 Capital, senior lecturer at Harvard Business School, and founding CRO at HubSpot

"Many excellent books on sales and sales methodologies exist. Many good books on leadership do too. But in this book, David Priemer has combined both into a roadmap to great sales leadership."

TONY RODONI, former executive vice president at Salesforce

"In *The Sales Leader They Need*, David Priemer artfully navigates the challenges and opportunities associated with balancing revenue growth and the true responsibility of leadership—helping people grow."

STEPHEN SHEDLETZKY, author of *Speak-Up Culture*

"If you're aiming to become the kind of sales leader that top talent fights to work with, David Priemer stands as an unparalleled mentor. Immersing yourself under his tutelage is akin to entering a dynamic sales laboratory, where complex concepts are not just simplified, but also masterfully unraveled. Emerging from this experience, you'll be equipped with precise tools and strategies, ready to elevate your sales leadership to new heights."

MIKE WOLFF, EVP and CRO of Salesforce.org

"David Priemer has done it again, and his timing is impeccable. His messages of transparency, accountability, and going all-in on caring for your sales team is so needed today. *The Sales Leader They Need* is a must-read for anyone aspiring to be a performance-achieving, science-backed, and people-centric leader."

JIM HAMILTON, Distinguished Faculty Fellow of sales management at the Smith School of Business, Queen's University

**The Sales Leader
They Need**

THE

SALES LEADER

THEY NEED

Five Critical Skills to Unlock Your Team's Potential

DAVID PRIEMER

●● PAGE TWO

Cataloguing in publication information is available
from Library and Archives Canada.
ISBN 978-1-77458-491-0 (paperback)
ISBN 978-1-77458-492-7 (ebook)

Page Two
pagetwo.com

Edited by James Harbeck
Copyedited by Jenny Govier
Proofread by Alison Strobel
Cover design by Peter Cocking
Interior design and illustrations
by Cameron McKague

cerebralselling.com

*To the courageous leaders who take on the weighty
responsibility of growing both revenue and people.*

Contents

Foreword

A S A SALES LEADER, how would you like the people on your team to remember you? As someone who did their job and worked to hit revenue targets? Someone who organized forecast calls, meetings, and a decent kickoff? Or would you like it better if they said you changed the way they do business, helped them discover more about themselves as a person, and developed the next generation of sales professionals and leaders?

I've had the honor of leading amazing, large-scale sales organizations for over twenty-five years and been responsible for delivering more than $1 billion in total revenue. In that time, I've worked with many outstanding sales leaders. I can tell you that the rewards both on and off the revenue dashboard for being a sales leader are tremendous. Unfortunately, there are scarcely few resources that provide a compass to that promised land. Many excellent books on sales and sales methodologies exist. Many good books on leadership do too. But in this book, David Priemer has combined both into a roadmap to great sales leadership.

David and I met many years ago when he was the vice president of sales at a software startup called Rypple. We ended up working together when Salesforce acquired his company. I can tell you that David is an incredible sales leader. And unique. As a former research scientist, David has an immense curiosity about not only the sales profession itself but also the hidden forces that drive it. He doesn't just ask "What?" to gain an operational understanding; he asks "Why?" and "How?" more than almost any other leader I've known. He understands that mastering the art and science of sales and sales leadership is all in the details. Not just the words and tactics but the tone, approach, and frameworks. His process taught me something about the fundamental difference between good sales leaders and great ones. Great sales leaders have a gift for synthesis. They find the recipe for success and write it down. They document the process. And in doing so, they uncover the hidden nuance that others miss.

As you use the ideas and frameworks in this book to build new sales leadership muscles and master the skills David so expertly presents, remember that this journey isn't meant to be easy. Bearing the load of both people leadership and massive quota responsibility is arguably the toughest combination in business. But to get it done and do it right, there is no substitute for putting in the reps and doing the work. After you do, I guarantee you'll be a better sales leader.

As I've often shared over the years, the hard way is the easy way. So it's time to get comfortable being uncomfortable and take up the journey to becoming the sales leader your team would fight to work with again. The sales leader they need.

TONY RODONI, former executive vice president, Salesforce

1

Foundations of Great Sales Leadership

That Wasn't in the Handbook

"What do you think we should do, David?"

When I was a vice president of sales at Salesforce, one of my sales managers came to me with a disturbing problem. He told me he had received a voicemail from a customer who didn't want to work with the female sales rep responsible for his account and requested we assign a male sales rep to help him instead.

I could see my manager was conflicted. On the one hand, what he really wanted to do was call the customer back and tell him off. But, of course, he was concerned about how the customer would respond and the subsequent fallout. Would the customer retaliate by sending a rage-induced email to our CEO, Marc Benioff? After all, as a customer-centric leader, Marc routinely shared his email address to provide an outlet for customers to contact him directly. And how would our segment react to losing a customer and the revenue that comes with them, even under these circumstances?

On the other hand, we dealt with problematic customers like this all the time, albeit rarely with this type of request. Maybe, in this case, the manager felt it would be easier to apologize profusely to the female rep for the customer's request, label his misogynistic behavior as completely inappropriate, but ultimately comply in the name of avoiding a confrontation.

No matter how detailed your onboarding manual or how comprehensive your ongoing professional development is, sooner or later every leader (and team member, for that matter) encounters a situation just like this: discrete scenarios that were somehow left out of the "how to be a sales leader" training manual, if those supports even exist. I'll tell you how we handled this one later in this chapter.

Eighty-three percent of organizations say that developing their leaders at all levels is important. Unfortunately, only 5 percent have actually made those investments. The trickle-down effect on the sales floor translates into leaders routinely burying their faces in their hands and lamenting things like these:

> "Why do I have to beg my team to keep their opportunities up to date in our CRM? And even when they do it, most of the time it feels like they're just going through the motions."

> "I know coaching my team and listening to their customer calls is important, but it's harder than I thought, and I don't spend as much time doing it as I should."

> "My team says they'll do things, but then they don't! How can I make sure everyone is accountable and does what they've committed to?"

> "I'm not sure my team is trying as hard as they can. How can I get them to care more and put in the extra effort we need to hit our sales targets?"

> "Feedback is so important when it comes to helping everyone get better, but getting and giving honest feedback is hard."

As our teams become more diverse and our workplaces increasingly virtual and distributed, leaders are encountering these scenarios with increasing frequency and complexity.

Yet the rewards for investing in ourselves as leaders are massive. A recent leadership development study spanning forty years of data from more than 18,000 leaders examined the bottom-line impact of making the right developmental investments. From a revenue perspective, the study showed a 114 percent increase in sales, a 233 percent increase in cross-selling, and a 300 percent increase in business referrals. This is in addition to a 71 percent increase in customer satisfaction, a 36 percent increase in productivity, a 77 percent decrease in turnover, and a 90 percent decrease in absenteeism.

So what magical sales leadership skills act as the key to helping you unlock this remarkable upside?

I'm about to show you that you already know the answer.

The Best Sales Leader You Ever Had

In my sales leadership training practice, I routinely kick things off by taking participants through a simple exercise. First, without any additional context or guidance, I ask them to recall the best sales leader they ever had. More than a few smiles emerge from the group as I ask them how long it took to settle on that individual. Interestingly, most of them report that the analysis was almost instantaneous, as though a single person leapt to mind when I asked them that question. More on the significance of that later.

Finally, we get to the most important part of the exercise, where I ask a critical question:

What was it about the best sales leader you ever had that made them so great?

Here I give participants a few moments to write their thoughts down. I would encourage you to stop here and do the same before reading on.

When I bring the group back together and ask them what types of things they had on their list, the details and themes are incredibly consistent across the thousands of leaders I've worked with. For example, I often see justifications like, "They were the best sales leader I ever had because they..."

· "pushed, challenged, and motivated me to be my best."

· "believed in me, saw my potential, and invested in my success."

· "listened to me, had my back, and guided my career."

· "coached me and gave me ongoing feedback."

· "helped me through a tough time in my life."

· "were empathetic, resourceful, and honest."

· "removed barriers and roadblocks for me and our team."

· "recognized the effort I and others put into our jobs."

· "were transparent and helped me understand their decisions."

· "held me and themselves accountable."

· "didn't micromanage and led by example."

Did you have any of these on your list?

What's interesting is that when you examine this list of the most common "best sales leader" criteria, you notice that almost all of the points can be summarized by two main themes:

1   **THEY CARED ABOUT ME:** They made me feel safe and important to them.

2 **THEY HELPED ME GROW:** I flourished personally and professionally under them.

Now, of course, doing these things likely helped you and your team achieve the business and revenue outcomes that were expected of you. But I suspect you'd agree that the motivation behind them wasn't simply for that leader to crush their quota. Instead, it came from their genuine desire to want to help you reach your full potential. It's also important to note that sentiments like caring, safety, and growth aren't meant to imply that top-shelf sales leadership is always administered with a warm smile and cheery disposition. Indeed, when others recall their favorite sales leaders, many share stories of how those leaders knew when tough love and unwavering accountability for results were in order. Yet, they felt those leaders always knew how to strike that delicate balance, earning the right to take a harder line when called for.

Equally as interesting and important is what you *don't* see on this list. For example, over thousands of data points, I have rarely had someone tell me that the best sales leader they ever had was also the best salesperson they ever knew. In fact, selling skills hardly ever come up. They weren't necessarily masters at crafting business cases, they weren't killer negotiators, nor did they give the best presentations or product demos. That's not to say they weren't great at those things. But rather, it wasn't those things that made them the best in the eyes of their team members. In the words of renowned business author and leadership guru Marshall Goldsmith, "What got you here won't get you there."

The skills you needed to become great at sales are not the same as the ones you need to become a great sales leader.

As a follow-on question to this exercise, I often ask leaders how they showed up for the best leader they ever had. In other words, what type of employee were they?

Not only do they report being hyper-engaged, going above and beyond, and being open and transparent with their own feelings with that leader, but they also had a strong desire to perform *for* that person. Sentiments like, "I tried so hard because I didn't want to disappoint them," or, "I would run through a brick wall for them!" were common. They were the type of leaders their team members would fight to work with again. And the science of great leadership backs this up.

The Science of Discretionary Effort

Suppose I asked you to rate yourself on a scale of one to ten with regard to the level of effort you're putting into your job. You would be a ten if you bleed company colors and have its logo tattooed on your shoulder. You would be a one if you've been checked out for weeks and have your resignation letter printed and ready to be turned in today. Where would you say you sit on that scale? If you're like most people, you're likely not a ten. After all, you have other interests, responsibilities, and distractions outside of work that are bound to consume at least some of your mental and operational bandwidth while on the job, right? Heck, even a nine or eight might be a stretch.

Now suppose you asked some of your team members the same question. What do you think they would say?

The reality is that, despite the quota pressures, healthy competition, and unbridled bravado we experience living in the sales trenches, most of us aren't giving everything we have at work. And neither is our team. That's normal. But what if you were able to get just a little bit more out of them? Even five or ten percentage points. That incremental boost in productivity is what I refer to as discretionary effort. It's the amount of extra intention, focus, and hustle that stems from a sense of engagement, caring, and safety created by you, a great sales leader. The specific skills and behaviors you need to unlock the potential of this discretionary effort are what we'll be exploring in this book. And while it might sound like magic, rest assured everything we'll be covering is firmly rooted in science.

A recent study examined the brain processes involved in recollections of resonant and dissonant leaders. Dissonant leaders are ones who have leadership styles or behaviors that are not in alignment or consistent with the goals and values of their team or organization. As a result, their behaviors may be viewed as ineffective, unproductive, or even harmful. Dissonant leadership can lead to negative outcomes such as decreased employee morale, job dissatisfaction, and reduced productivity. On the other hand, "resonant leaders" are in lockstep with the goals and values of the team or organization and are often viewed as effective and productive.

The study examined the brain processes involved in recollections of interactions with both types of leaders, and brain scans using functional magnetic resonance imaging (fMRI) were subsequently performed using stimuli derived from these memories. Recalling a dissonant leader resulted in heightened activity in regions of the brain linked to evasion and negative emotions—and the opposite was true for a resonant leader.

Results from another study by researchers at the University of Michigan and Cornell University suggest that leaders who show empathy toward their teams can help build both personal and team resilience during periods of adversity. In yet another study of 1,500 workers from Australia, China, Germany, India, Mexico, and the United States, psychologists Jeanine Prime and Elizabeth Salib found that observing altruistic or selfless behavior in their leaders was one of the key factors contributing to employees going above and beyond the call of duty. Not only that, but the increased levels of engagement also came with a boost in the areas of innovation and process improvement.

So caring about your team members and helping them grow personally and professionally is the key to unlocking this tremendous value. This book will show you how to package up "caring and growth" into a consistent set of skills and repeatable behaviors to allow you to do just that.

Your 3-Point Sales Leadership Self-Assessment

Before we get into a discussion of leadership skills you need to master in order to drive these results, it's important to understand the opportunities you have for growth in three key areas of your leadership practice. In other words, what are some of the principles that make it hard to be a great leader?

1. Focus

At my companies, we routinely surveyed our team members to get feedback on the effectiveness of our leadership and management style (more on this survey in chapter 6). The quarterly exercise featured a short list of questions that included, "What is one thing your manager could do more of? And less of?"

The insights gathered from this particular two-part question were powerful because they had to do with how we, as leaders, spend our limited time. Indeed, in a world full of infinite distractions, quotas, deadlines, and the need to maintain our personal sanity, many leaders struggle with time management.

For example, most sales leaders and their teams agree more time should be spent coaching reps, shadowing them in customer meetings, delegating, and carrying out other strategic planning that helps the operation grow. On the flip side, they'd like to spend less time sitting in unfocused meetings, jumping into deals, and generally taking a reactive approach to the daily menu of issues and problems.

So the question for you is, as a leader, what would you like to be doing more of and less of in your role?

To help you along, draw a simple two-column chart like the one below, think for a few moments, and start listing as many things as you can before continuing.

I'd like to do more . . .	I'd like to do less . . .

Having run this exercise with thousands of leaders, I have seen common themes emerge.

Great leaders want to spend more quality time with their team members. They know that developing high-potential people and delegating important tasks can be a huge cultural and time-saving multiplier when it comes to achieving their goals. They want to coach, motivate, and thank their people more consistently for the great work they do and do a better job of promoting those winning behaviors across their team and organization so people can replicate them. They want to spend more time planning and strategizing, laying the foundation for greater levels of individual and team productivity. And they want to spend more time driving accountability, ensuring people live up to the commitments they make to each other and do what they say they're going to do.

So what's preventing them (and you) from doing more of the things they want to do?

One of the biggest barriers is simply the nature of the modern workplace. Leaders unanimously report being overscheduled and sitting in unproductive meetings on a daily basis. The irony is that during the COVID-19 pandemic, more than 75 percent of workers reported that working from home resulted in time savings due to a reduction in commute times and business travel. But the modern, hybrid work environment exacerbated the already problematic issue of time management. Interactions that used to take place quickly in hallways, break rooms, and over-the-shoulder chit-chat have been replaced by formal meetings and scheduled conversations. In fact, data from the enterprise software firm Atlassian shows the average workday has expanded by a full thirty minutes globally, no doubt as a result of meeting overload. In response to this negative trend, some companies have been forced to take drastic measures. For example, e-commerce giant Shopify outright banned recurring meetings involving two or more employees in order to preserve precious work time.

As a result of these time constraints, leaders report having inconsistent one-on-one coaching sessions and being more reactive when it comes to addressing problems in their operations. Attention, bandwidth, and sanity are in short supply, which causes leaders to begrudgingly regress into a more directive management style. In other words, when we don't have time to coach our teams, guide them to the answers they need, and help them figure out the solutions to their problems on their own, we simply tell them what to do—a behavior that serves neither of us in the long run.

The good news is that the first step in addressing your issues of focus is simply being mindful of how you're spending your time today and where you'd like to place more attention. With that in mind, let's turn our attention to the second part of your self-assessment.

2. Trust

Most would agree that trust is a foundational principle of both the practice of sales and sales leadership. And leaders' actions are filtered and interpreted by our team members through the lens of trust. Thinking back to the "best sales leader you ever had" exercise, you'll recall that most respondents reported that their leader challenged them to be the best version of themselves. But if you didn't trust that leader or feel they cared about you, you might consider their act of challenging you directly punitive or antagonistic. In fact, in her book *Radical Candor*, author and CEO coach Kim Scott refers to this mode of discourse as "Obnoxious Aggression." For that reason, trust is seen as a leading indicator of whether a leader's team will have a positive or negative impression of them.

But how is trust actually built?

A 2019 study by Jack Zenger and Joseph Folkman examined the data from the 360-degree assessments of 87,000 leaders. Their analysis uncovered three key factors that form the foundation for trust:

1 **POSITIVE RELATIONSHIPS:** Is the leader able to create positive relationships with other people and groups within their organization?

2 **GOOD JUDGMENT/EXPERTISE:** Is the leader well-informed and knowledgeable about the technical aspects of their team members' roles?

3 **CONSISTENCY:** Does the leader follow through on their commitments and do what they say they will do?

The researchers were also curious as to whether leaders needed to be equally proficient in all three elements or if one had a more significant impact than the others. In the end, it was the impact of having positive relationships with others that reigned supreme. In fact, even in the absence of good judgment and consistency, having positive relationships engendered the highest levels of trust. That means the reverse is also true. If the relationship between you and your team members is damaged or never existed, trust is difficult to establish.

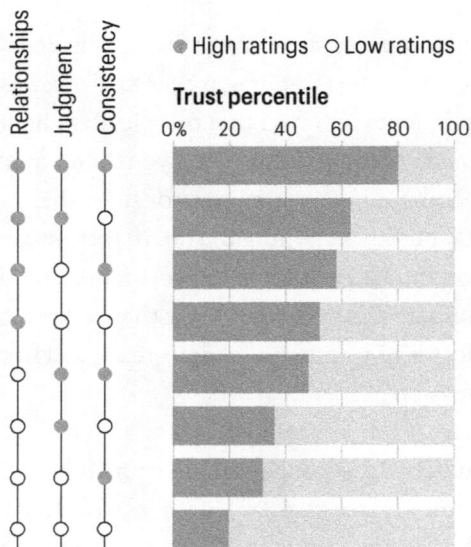

Source: Jack Zenger and Joseph Folkman, "The 3 Elements of Trust," *Harvard Business Review,* February 5, 2019, hbr.org/2019/02/the-3-elements-of-trust.

The same researchers also examined the role of warmth and likability as they relate to relationships, trust, and overall leadership effectiveness, in many ways reframing political theorist Machiavelli's question, "Is it better to be loved or feared?" In the hit TV show *The Office,* manager Michael Scott, played by Steve Carell, asks the very same question and quickly concludes, "Easy. Both. I want people to be afraid of how much they love me." As it turns out, he's not entirely wrong!

Evidence suggests that if our goal as leaders is to leverage the power of relationships to guide and influence, feelings of warmth and likability are the surest road to victory. Being likable improves the quality of our relationships and the trust that underpins them in part because it enhances the absorption of ideas. In other words, when people like us, they're more likely to view our suggestions as helpful and productive. When you're a leader, this contributes to their perception of your effectiveness. Not surprisingly, out of 51,836 leaders studied, only 27 were rated poorly in likability but highly in leadership effectiveness. That means that the likelihood of an unpopular manager being considered a successful leader is very low—about 0.05 percent, or 1 in 2,000.

To help you begin to assess the level of trust and the quality of the relationship between you and your team members, here's a quick exercise.

Consider the following questions:

1　Does my team feel I have their back?

2　Does my team feel I care about them personally?

3　Does my team feel I understand their strengths and opportunities for development?

4　Would my team fight to work with me again?

Now draw a two-axis chart like the one in the following relationship matrix. The vertical axis represents the strength of the sentiment, and the horizontal axis represents the consistency of that sentiment across the team. For example, the position of the "2" in the chart shows that the leader it describes believes that most of their team feels they generally care about them personally, but the position of the "3" shows that they may not have the clearest sense of their team members' unique strengths and areas for development. Take a moment and plot out where you might sit on this chart with respect to the four questions.

An even more telling exercise would be to ask your team these same questions. That's what we'll be exploring further in chapter 6. For now, if you feel there's an opportunity to strengthen the foundation of trust in your relationships or do it more consistently across your team, keep reading. The five core leadership skills we'll be exploring in the chapters to follow will help you do just that.

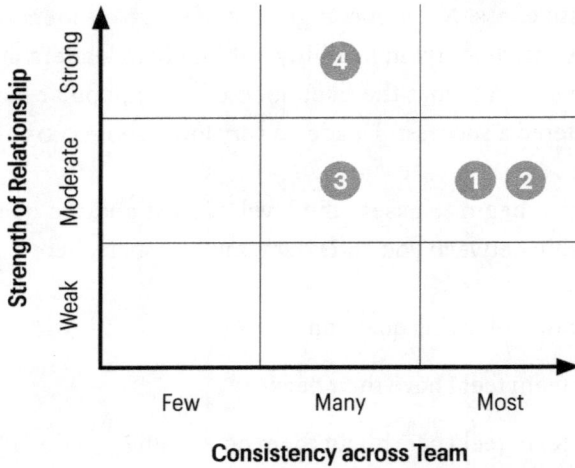

When it comes to driving revenue, trusting relationships are more critical than you might think. This became painfully obvious to me back at Salesforce when I joined the organization after they acquired my third startup in 2012. The transition from leading a sales team at a 45-person company to a 6,000-employee global player was jarring. The people, culture, and opportunity were amazing. But operationally, the experience felt like making the leap from a small-town high school to a big-city university.

Overnight, helping my team get even basic deals done became incredibly complex. The agility and contracting flexibility we once enjoyed had evaporated. We were no longer able to provide our customers with the same type of commercial and legal concessions we once did. Our core master service agreement was rigid, and giving customers any leeway to modify its terms was discouraged. Changes were strictly controlled, and the approval process was both rigorous and time-consuming. Making modifications to certain payment and billing terms proved equally laborious, requiring special approval from our sales operations team. As we saw our deal cycles become longer and more complex, my team became understandably frustrated. I quickly realized I needed to make new friends at the company—friends who knew the ropes and could help me figure out how to operate in this new environment with maximum speed and minimal friction. As it turned out, my survival strategy is backed by research.

In a sales effectiveness study of a large B2B software company, workplace analytics expert Ryan Fuller uncovered some fascinating insights consistent with my experience. After looking at sales data from across the entire global organization, he found that regardless of what products their reps were selling, the type and size of organizations they were selling to, or where in the world they were located, revenue production was highly correlated with three things:

1   Spending enough time with customers and prospects
2   Getting coaching and mentorship from the leaders in your own organization
3   Having a large and healthy network in your own organization

While points one and two may seem intuitive (and rest assured we'll be exploring the second one in chapter 5), the third one is often overlooked but extremely important. As our organizations become increasingly complex, learning how to efficiently navigate them to get deals approved internally is critical to minimizing the friction for both your team and your customers.

Fuller's data shows that as the number of weeks left in a given quarter decreases, the time spent with customers actually starts to decline. At the same time, top performers rely on strong internal connections to bring their deals to fruition. This means that, as a leader, if you're not able to forge a network of healthy relationships with key players within your own organization to support you, your team and overall revenue attainment will suffer.

Number of Strong
Internal Connections

Hours per Week in
Meetings with Prospects

Internal network size steadily increases
and peaks near quarter end

Time with customers starts high
and declines as quarter end nears

Weeks until End of Quarter

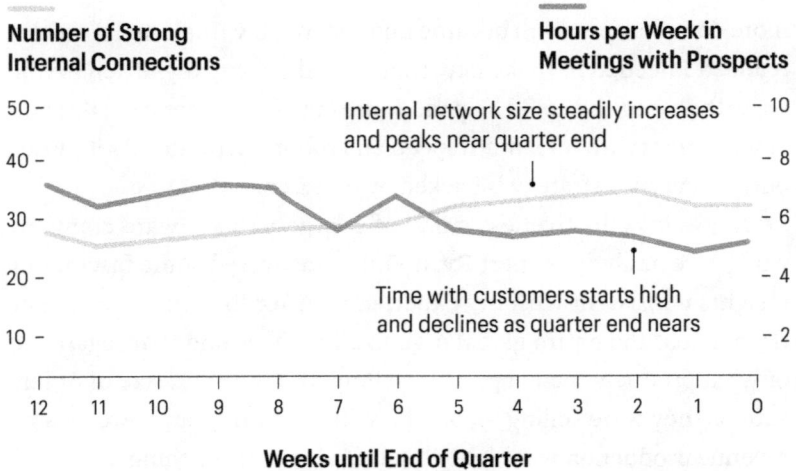

Source: Ryan Fuller, "3 Behaviors That Drive Successful Salespeople," *Harvard Business Review*, August 20, 2014, hbr.org/2014/08/3-behaviors-that-drive-successful-salespeople.

These relationships can also be exceptionally beneficial even outside of high-pressure sales periods. For example, when prospects would ask my reps for a reference call with an existing customer, we would sometimes position a conversation with one of our customer success or implementation leaders as a quicker and more effective way of addressing their concerns. In other instances, we would call on one of our product managers or engineers to field customer questions about our product roadmaps or integration strategy. And on some occasions, we may have needed to twist the arm of our legal counsel or CEO to dispense a little more commercial flexibility to get a deal in a struggling sales territory over the finish line.

Fortunately, developing these relationships isn't difficult, but it does require intentional effort on your part. For example, you might consider grabbing a coffee or lunch with an experienced peer or leader at your company and have them share some of the key lessons learned along their journey. As you do, ask if they don't mind if you hit them up with questions as you work through any unfamiliar internal processes. To deepen your relationship with key internal stakeholders such as finance, legal, or IT, consider inviting them to a one-on-one meeting where you ask them for feedback on ways they feel your teams can work better together. Doing this in advance of needing their help shows them you respect the value they add to your revenue operation and appreciate their insights.

As a sales leader, it's important for you to be honest with yourself about the quality and breadth of relationships you have across your organization and ask yourself two key questions:

1   Which stakeholders or departments do I need to cultivate strong relationships with that perhaps I haven't already?

2   How might I leverage the power of these relationships to help my team sell more in ways I may not have considered?

3. Predictability

When we think about the qualities of great leaders, we often think about traits like compassion, intelligence, empathy, and honesty. But one of the more critical leadership qualities is also one of the most boring: predictability. In fact, it's often said that the best leaders are the most predictable, and for good reason. By being able to anticipate our thoughts, actions, and decisions, our teams can behave in a manner consistent with them, even when we're not around. This is especially true in the sales trenches, where reps need to make dozens of customer- and opportunity-related decisions on a daily basis, often on the fly.

If you think back to your childhood, you can probably remember things you did that drove your parents or caregiver absolutely mad. Maybe it was leaving your room in a constant state of disaster, ditching your dirty dishes in the sink, being sent to the principal's office at school, or sneaking home after your curfew. The same principles apply in the realm of sales leadership.

As a leader, you probably have a certain code of team behaviors, principles, and ethics you abide by. It might be expecting a certain level of prospecting activity or hustle from your reps. It might be ensuring that your team's opportunities are constantly accurate and up to date in your customer relationship management (CRM) system (we used to refer to this as "real-time all the time"). Or you might have certain standards for the amount of practice and preparation that goes into delivering presentations to customer executives. On the flip side, there might be certain behaviors and expectations that your team's former leaders had that you don't. For example, you may not expect your team to go into every customer interaction with full knowledge of your product roadmap. You might be flexible on what point during the sales cycle your reps provide customers with pricing proposals. Or you might be OK with your reps choosing to opt out of team meetings if they have an important customer meeting to attend to.

If I pulled a handful of your team members aside and asked them about the behaviors you expect of them, are you predictable enough that they would know? What might they say?

Regardless of what your expectations are, creating awareness about them can help your team operate more consistently and make decisions quicker. The problem is, as leaders, we're not always clear about what these things are, either explicitly to our teams or even in our own minds. This results in wasted effort and mutual frustration when engaging in the wrong or bad behaviors inevitably triggers a negative reaction.

When Is It OK to Fail?

The first step in becoming a more predictable leader is to be clear about the things that are OK for your team to mess up and the things that aren't. I call this the #Fail exercise. To help crystalize these insights, draw a simple two-column chart like the one below, think for a few moments, and list at least three items in each category before continuing. Of course, you can list more if you like, but the goal of this exercise is to make it easy for your team to remember what these things are, so the more focused you can be, the better.

OK to #Fail	Not OK to #Fail
1.	1.
2.	2.
3.	3.

Once you have your items listed, the next step is to explicitly communicate them to your team. Keep in mind that the exercise of sharing these insights should never feel forced or punitive. People prefer alignment and clarity to uncertainty and friction, which is why your team *wants* to know what these things are—for the same reasons you want to share them.

Back in my last role as VP of sales, I made these expectations an explicit part of my own onboarding processes. In fact, on my very first day on the job, I held an all-hands meeting with my team of thirty-five reps. After some warm introductions and sharing my excitement for the opportunity, I added, with a smile, "Now, I know many of you have probably been doing your own background checks on me through your network over the last little while. You're probably trying to 'figure me out,' and I think that's great! My goal is to help by being as transparent and predictable as I can." I started by sharing more about my background and family life. Then I transitioned to the things I love: brands, ideas, and hobbies. Finally, I laid out the three core values I felt it was important for us to embody as a team. I explained why they were important for us at the stage we were at (more on why that was important later) and provided examples of behaviors that align with those values. The more tangible and explicit I could be, the better. And the same goes for you.

To punctuate the value of predictability, let's turn our attention back to the story from the beginning of this chapter. One of the managers on my team was deciding how to handle their customer's request to swap their female sales rep out for a male. Recognizing that one of his fears was the potential fallout if the customer decided to escalate their frustration to our CEO, I asked him a simple question: "If our CEO was a sales manager here and happened to find himself in exactly the same situation as you, what do you think he would do?"

Marc was a very predictable leader, and his beliefs were both tightly held and widely visible across not only the organization but also the business community at large, particularly in the area of equality. At that moment the answer became abundantly clear to the manager.

He called the customer back and without any fear or hesitation said, "It's too bad you don't want to work with your rep. She's one of the best and most experienced in our segment, and you're lucky to have her. But if you don't want to work with a woman, Salesforce is probably not the company you want to be doing business with."

We never heard from the customer again.

Five Sales Leadership Skills to Master

At this point, I hope you have a sense of the tremendous, and some-times hidden, upside of being the best sales leader your team ever had: more revenue, faster growth, increases in productivity and dis-cretionary effort, and a high-affinity team that would assemble and fight alongside you like an army of Marvel superheroes wherever you all might land in the future. Of course, none of this will happen by accident!

The first step is to be honest with yourself as to where you stand today when it comes to winning the hearts and minds of your sales reps.

1 **FOCUS**: Are you clear on the things you should be doing more of and less of in your role to serve your team?

2 **TRUST**: Are the relationships with your team members and key stakeholders built on a deep sense of caring?

3 **PREDICTABILITY**: Is the culture of your team clear enough for your people to know how to execute when you're not watching?

Every sales leader, regardless of experience or tenure, can find opportunities to grow in one or more of these areas. The key is looking at these opportunities through the lens of the five foundational skills we'll be exploring in the chapters ahead:

1 **PROMOTING TRANSPARENCY**: Providing the "why" to go with the "what" to help your team act with greater purpose and be more invested in the outcome.

2 **PROTECTING AND ADVOCATING**: Demonstrating to your team that you have their back, to create a circle of safety and unlock higher levels of discretionary effort.

3 **DRIVING ACCOUNTABILITY:** Making sure everyone does the things they've committed to doing for the company and each other.

4 **COACHING YOUR TEAM:** Diagnosing and fixing execution and operational issues in your sales funnel to drive growth and continuous improvement.

5 **GETTING AND GIVING FEEDBACK:** Sourcing the insights both you and your team need to learn fast and win.

So if you're ready to be that sales leader who leaves an indelible mark on the lives and careers of their teams forever, grab your super suit, and let's get started!

2

SKILL 1

Promoting Transparency

That Damn CRM!

Do you know that if someone asked you, "What's the weather going to be like tomorrow?" and you answered, "Pretty much like today," you'd have a 70 percent chance of being right?

This was one of the more humbling lessons my friend Chris Scott and I learned as we sat in an undergraduate synoptic meteorology lecture together back in 1997. Chris's fascination with weather took root on August 8, 1983, when tennis-ball-sized hail stones rocketed down on his family's farm, destroying their crops. That fascination turned to passion, and years later he became the chief meteorologist at the Weather Network. I also earned a certificate in meteorology and spent the first part of my career as a research scientist—but then my path took an ironic entrepreneurial twist, resulting in almost twenty years as a B2B sales leader. More on how that path unfolded in chapter 7, but for now, let the jokes about "forecast accuracy" fly.

The truth is, weather forecasting and sales forecasting aren't all that different. They both involve crunching a lot of variables and harmonizing empirical data with mathematical models, and both are much more accurate in the short term than the long term. They are also similar in that the accuracy of the forecast depends on the quality of the data that goes into it. Cue the collective groan from sales leaders across the globe who *swear* they'd be able to absolutely nail their revenue forecasts if they could only get their reps to keep their opportunity details up to date in that damn CRM!

As a sales leader, you could probably fill a book with the excuses your reps give you for why the data in the CRM isn't correct.

"Oh sorry, yeah ... I still need to do a bit of forecast clean-up there."

"Those opportunities were logged by the last rep in my territory, but I don't think they're real."

"Yeah, I forgot the deal value on that opportunity was based on our list price, and there's no way the customer will pay that."

"Wouldn't you rather I spend my time actually selling than doing admin work?"

If ensuring your systems are filled with accurate and timely sales opportunity data is a core expectation of your reps' jobs, why do we spend so much time and energy reminding them? Why can't they appreciate how important it is and just *do* it?

Nancy Duarte is a bestselling author who has spent over thirty years as a CEO and leads the largest design firm in Silicon Valley. In her business, she's constantly helping leaders and organizations figure out how to persuade their audiences to get on board with a new idea, operating model, or change in behavior. Her high-profile and sophisticated clients are very clear about the impact they want to have in their respective markets and how that change needs to happen. The question they've rarely considered is this: *Why* would their customers actually want to change their behavior? Your team is no different.

Consider for a moment that any extra work or task you ask your team to complete outside of direct selling activities will be seen as a chore—something they don't see immediate value in doing, even if it's technically considered part of their core job. This can be true for tactical requests like attending a weekly meeting or driving registration to a marketing event, but it's especially true for administrative tasks like CRM upkeep. And when you ask your team to do one of these things, it's unlikely their first question (whether spoken or not) will be about *how* that work might get done. Rather, they'll ask *why* it needs to be done. In other words, tactical details like what the email invitations should look like, what the meeting agenda should be, or how to format their monthly forecasts are secondary considerations. First, we need to sufficiently motivate our teams to perform the task. We need them to engage.

Engaged Salespeople Drive Revenue

The Gallup organization defines engagement as the involvement and enthusiasm of employees in both their work and their workplace. Put another way, it describes how much they care about what they do and how hard they try to do it. Sadly, according to Gallup's *State of the Global Workplace: 2023 Report*, only about one in five employees globally is engaged at work. And employees who fall into the categories of "not engaged" or "actively disengaged" cost the world $8.8 trillion in lost productivity, or approximately 9 percent of global GDP. These statistics are especially poignant because they relate to sales and revenue growth.

The same organization conducted a meta-analysis aggregating the findings from hundreds of research studies. They found that companies with the highest level of employee engagement had 21 percent higher levels of overall profitability. A different longitudinal study on employee engagement by Harvard business professor James Heskett tracked 200 companies over the course of eleven years. He found that companies with a strong corporate culture that included engagement initiatives grew their revenue 682 percent over the course of that period. Even a study of car rental sales reps by Yale University researchers demonstrated that engaged employees were more successfully able to upsell clients to more expensive vehicles and higher rates. The result was not only increased revenue for the business but also happier and more satisfied customers. The bottom line is this: engaged sales teams drive more sales and higher profits than disengaged teams. So the question is, How can you get more of these engaged sellers?

Fortunately, engagement isn't a characteristic you have to worry about hiring for. Engaged salespeople are created. Like diamonds that form over the course of time under the right conditions of pressure and temperature, engaged sellers are formed by their leaders, teammates, and organizations in the right environments. But promoting engagement isn't about lavishing your salespeople with material or financial benefits like lucrative compensation plans. If it were, salespeople would be consistently lured away to work for other companies by the promise of more pay, commissions, and bonuses. While financial incentives can certainly grab salespeople's attention, experienced sellers know not to take the bait. The grass on the other side is rarely as green as it seems. Like all employees, the best salespeople crave environments where they can make a real impact while growing personally and professionally.

One of the most powerful ways to engage a salesperson is simply to help them establish a psychological or emotional connection to their work. You can do this by helping them understand *why* they're being asked to do something and the importance of that task to both their growth and that of the business. By operating with a high degree of transparency, your team is more likely to put a greater degree of intention behind their work. Without transparency, we reduce meaningful work to a series of tasks, the results of which they ultimately care less about.

Invoking the Power of Transparency

Mastering the why is one of the most powerful skills we can model as leaders. Here are five ways to do that.

1. Share Insights into How and Why the Business Runs

A study by McKinsey & Company found that 70 percent of employees say their sense of purpose is defined by their work. At the same time, the COVID-19 pandemic caused nearly half of Americans to reconsider the kind of work they do. Millennials, who are forecasted to make up 75 percent of the workforce by 2030, are three times more likely than other groups to put their jobs under the microscope.

That means that one of the ways sales leaders can help their teams find purpose in their work is to connect their actions to the mission of the organization and the outcomes they drive. In fact, many employees have a strong desire to be connected to the business and understand both how and why it runs. The transparency you create with your insights and perspectives can play a big part in that.

Back in 2016, Mike Wolff was the senior vice president of sales at Salesforce, running the core small business segment for the Americas. With hundreds of sales reps and managers in his charge, ensuring that our collective CRM data was accurate, clean, and up to date was critical to running this large portion of our business. To ensure his team acted with purpose, he would often share public notes like this one, which he posted to our internal network at the end of one August sales period:

Every month, as we close out our current month and prepare to quickly transition to the next month, we ask everyone to look at their sixty-day pipeline and ensure that it's clean.

Oftentimes, I receive such feedback as, "Yep, Mike, my pipeline is clean," "I'm on it," and "What does 'clean' mean?"

For a number of reasons, this is an important part of our business. For instance, our Marketing organization makes investment decisions based on the health of our pipeline, budgets for local events are allocated, resource decisions are made, and, most importantly, having an accurate pipeline ensures we make the most of our time and understand where to focus our day-to-day efforts.

Therefore, as we finish August strong and prepare for September, thank you for reviewing the attached "Rinse and Repeat" checklist and updating/cleaning your sixty-day pipeline.

One of my former sales reps, Sammy Singh, who is now an accomplished sales leader, was faced with a similar problem. The revenue expectations of the business had increased, which meant his sales team could no longer rely solely on the inbound leads coming from their marketing department to generate enough pipeline to hit their targets. His reps would have to do more of their own outbound prospecting. For a team that had grown accustomed to not having to do much prospecting, this was an uphill battle. They complained that inbound leads closed much quicker than outbound leads and that spending too much time prospecting would be a fruitless drain on their bandwidth.

Instead of arguing with his team, Sammy decided to dive into the sales data to create the transparency needed to make his case. He found that while deals sourced from outbound prospecting activities indeed took an average of 17 percent more time to close, their typical revenue size was three times larger than that of inbound-sourced opportunities. The team agreed that the investment of a little more time and effort for a lot more revenue suddenly sounded good, and their prospecting activities intensified.

Research shows that providing this type of transparency creates a deeper connection between your team's actions and business outcomes, boosting their productivity. What's more, connected employees are healthier, more engaged, and more resilient in the face of adversity, they have a stronger sense of loyalty, and they stay at the company longer.

2. Explain How Their Efforts Allow You to Advocate for Them

One of the most powerful ways to show your team you have their back and unlock their discretionary effort is to advocate for them. In other words, understand the key things holding them back and work to remove those roadblocks where you can. We'll be discussing this concept in more detail in chapter 3. For now, suppose you wanted to leverage the power of transparency to boost your team's sense of purpose when it comes to getting them to keep their opportunity data up to date in your CRM. Consider showing them the reports and forecasts their data fuels and explain how you present those up the chain to your leadership, executive team, or board of directors. Underscore that the more accurate that information is, the better the position you'll be in to influence the organizational decisions that impact them the most—such as hiring, compensation planning, and investments in marketing and sales support.

In my last role as VP of sales, I would routinely show my team members the presentations I was asked to deliver to our executive leadership and board illustrating the state of our sales organization. As I did, I would point out specific trends and patterns in the data from our CRM and how they were interpreted and delivered to those key players to drive the importance of this message home. In some cases,

I would even outline the narratives the data was leading me toward *before* delivering them up the chain. That allowed my team to intercept any inaccurate conclusions and make any necessary adjustments in the CRM to reflect the true state of our business.

For example, in one particular business review, the board asked how I felt about our pipeline coverage for the upcoming quarter. While the average sales cycle length for our solution was about 65 days, the average age of the pipeline in the coming month was 95 days. The same statistic was 125 days two months out. I explained to the team that, for someone looking at these pipeline statistics without context, they might assume our upcoming deal roster was full of stale, poorly executed opportunities that were pushed from previous sales periods. While—let's be honest—there's always some of that in every sales forecast, the team's diligent CRM hygiene allowed me to showcase to the board that this period also included a number of large enterprise opportunities that had naturally longer sales cycles. As a result, they were skewing both our pipeline coverage and cycle length statistics. As for the team, they clearly understood and appreciated the importance of keeping their opportunity rigor tight when it came to defending their performance up the chain.

3. Make Instructions More Actionable

One of the reasons our teams fail to complete tasks in the manner in which we expect them to is that we aren't clear about what specifically we want them to do. Instructions like "Make sure your opportunities are up to date in the CRM," "Be sure you make fifteen prospecting calls today," or even "Please get that executive presentation ready to go by Tuesday" are vague and can be interpreted in many different ways.

For example, most CRM opportunities have dozens of fields. Do *all* of them have to be 100 percent accurate? When you ask your reps to make fifteen prospecting calls, can they be to any prospects the rep chooses, or should they be focused on a specific title, persona, geography, or solution set? Maybe "calls" isn't really what we mean, since leaving fifteen voicemails doesn't often translate into pipeline production. Perhaps we should be clearer and tell them "call connects" (i.e., when the customer actually answered the phone and they had a conversation) is the success metric we're after.

To minimize confusion and promote focused effort, the more transparent and specific you can be about how the task should be completed, the better. For example, at Salesforce, when we asked reps to ensure their opportunity details were up to date, we clarified that what we were after was accuracy and completeness over the next sixty days in four fields:

1 **ANNUAL CONTRACT VALUE:** How much revenue do we expect this opportunity to generate each year? This should become more accurate the closer we get to the close date.

2 **CLOSE DATE:** What specific date are we expecting contract signatures to occur on? Month-end dates were generally acceptable here since we forecasted monthly, but this should become more specific as we get closer to the date.

3 **STAGE:** Where is this deal sitting in the pipeline? We had defined an eight-stage sales process with specific exit criteria for each to ensure we had a common language for deal progression.

4 **NEXT STEPS:** What has the customer agreed to do with us next in order to move the deal forward? For example, a good next step would be "Call set at 10 AM on November 4 to review the proposal with the CEO." Next steps should not be an aspirational take on what we *want* them to be (e.g., "Get executives to a demo"). If the customer hasn't agreed to do anything, the next step should be about our plan to get that in place. For example, "Customer gone dark. Jennifer, our VP, will be placing a call to their CEO on May 17 to get the conversation moving again."

Creating transparency about your requests by making them specific not only makes them more actionable but also puts you in a much better position to hold your team accountable for the outcome you're looking for. We'll be exploring the accountability skill in greater detail in chapter 4.

4. Show Them What "Good" Looks Like

In 2016, under the direction of our new COO, Salesforce decided to increase its prices for the first time in its history. That meant that for new customers, the monthly license fee for a single Sales Cloud user increased from $125 per month to $150. Of course, some members of the sales team were worried that a 20 percent price increase might scare off budget-conscious prospects who already saw us as a premium solution. This was especially true in the small business segment I led. To help cushion the blow, leadership agreed that the price increase wouldn't be introduced immediately for new customers but rather would take effect in two months' time.

Marching orders to the sales team were clear: "There's no immediate impact for current customers with existing contracts. But call your prospects who might be sitting on the fence and tell them the price is going up for the first time ever. Since the increase won't take effect for two more months, there's never been a better time to buy. If they sign up now, they can lock in at the lower rate."

This sounded like a winning strategy. Salespeople are always looking for a compelling reason to kickstart a conversation with prospects, and "There's never been a better time to buy" felt like a message that could be delivered with high conviction. Unfortunately, the approach resulted in a lot more irate prospects than we expected. Puzzled, we dug in and tried to figure out what was going wrong. As it turned out, the reps were delivering the right message, but their tone and approach had all the finesse of an elephant attempting to try on lingerie. It sounded shlocky, as though the reps were making up the story of the price increase just to push customers to buy—a narrative that invoked all the negative associations buyers have of salespeople. Not the experience we were hoping for.

We realized that we had told the reps *what* to do, but we had never shown them what a good version of someone delivering the message sounded like.

In 2017, as the VP of sales at another software company, I faced a similar challenge. We were phasing out one of our most popular pricing plans. As before, we decided to give prospective customers a couple of months to choose to move forward before we did. But having learned from my previous experience, I decided to take a different approach. Instead of giving high-level instructions, writing out the call script in a document, or sharing the details in a team meeting, I had one of my enterprise sales leaders practice delivering the narrative several times. As he did, he fine-tuned both the words and tone until they sounded perfect. I then asked him to record himself delivering it and shared the recording with the team. "Do it just like that!" we said. With the nuance of the tone and approach crystalized, the team had a blueprint they could easily practice and emulate. The result was zero customer complaints and the highest-revenue quarter in company history.

You can do the very same thing with many of your sales tools and processes, from your intro presentation and product demo scripts to your discovery and objection-handling playbooks. When you invoke the power of transparency by showing your team what good looks like, you'll not only drive the outcomes you want more consistently but also show your team you care by setting them up for maximum success.

5. Be Honest about What You Think

During my first tour as a sales leader, I learned an important lesson about transparency the hard way. I was twenty-five years old when I joined my first startup as a solutions engineer and employee number twenty. Seven years later, the company had grown into a $100 million business with 700 employees and had an IPO along the way. At that point, I was the senior director of solutions consulting and led a team of twenty-one amazing people, many of whom I became good friends with. Shortly thereafter, we went through a turbulent acquisition by a much larger company. About one-third of my company was let go, including our entire senior leadership and a few members of my team. The cultural and operational differences between our two companies were stark, and I could tell that my remaining crew was trying to decide if they should stay the course or leave for greener pastures. I was conflicted.

On the one hand, I shared their concerns and feared the uncertainty in the months ahead. On the other, the new ownership wanted me to stay on, keep my team focused and productive, and help educate the larger organization on our value to the now vastly expanded customer base. In the end, I tried my best to focus on the positives and align everyone with the opportunity that lay before us.

Not surprisingly, the next couple of months were stressful as I watched a number of my team members tender their resignations one by one. During that time, my friend and marketing director, who was close with many people on my team, approached me with some feedback. "Just so you know," she said, "your team doesn't feel you're being completely honest with them. They see you trying to put on a brave face, but they think you're just as concerned about what's going on as they are. They wish you'd share more about what you're thinking with them." She was right.

Being calm, optimistic, reassuring, and willing to tackle new challenges are prized traits in a leader, especially during times of adversity. However, so is being human. In the face of uncertainty, a lack of transparency and an unwillingness to address the elephant in the room can erode the trust between you and your team, damaging those relationships and creating unnecessary stress. While overshar-ing can be equally problematic, especially when the path forward is unclear, being up front and honest with your team about how you feel will strengthen your bond with them. Never lose your team's trust.

The Need for Certainty

Have you ever experienced the agonizing feeling of waiting for the results of an important medical test like an X-ray, ultrasound, or MRI? As a cancer survivor, I have. Many times, and still do. The anxiety builds with each passing moment, blocking out rational thoughts as your mind races to contemplate, "What could this thing be?" "Why could it be taking so long?" or "What happens if it comes back posi-tive?" This is our brain's search for one of the most primal, critical, and satisfying emotions: certainty.

Humans crave certainty, from our days crowding in caves and around campfires, wondering if our tribe had enough resources to survive the cold winter ahead. Or in our ancestral homes, hoping our leaders had the might to defend us against invaders while we slept. Without certainty, our brains are forced into a frantic search for answers, trying to see our way to a finish line amidst variables we don't control and knowledge we don't possess. But when it arrives, a biochemical cocktail of hormones comes with it, making us feel at ease and secure.

One of the reasons transparency is such a powerful driver of trust and affinity is that it helps create certainty in the minds of our teams. Our brains are prediction machines, which is why uncertainty makes us do funny things. As the saying goes, "We suffer more in imagina-tion than in reality." Your team is no exception. Sales is a competitive, anxiety-riddled, and emotional roller coaster at the best of times. Throw in a pandemic, economic uncertainty, a turbulent venture funding market, industry consolidation, or fear-driven layoffs and it's easy for salespeople to get caught up in "what ifs" and worst-case scenarios:

- What if we can't raise that next round of funding?
- Why can't my boss see that I'm ready for a promotion?
- What will next year's comp plan look like?
- Why aren't I getting any good leads?
- Will territories get smaller as we hire more sales reps?
- I hope that client doesn't ghost me, or my quarterly forecast is shot!

Our minds are dizzy trying to consider all the variables as we ruminate over every possible outcome, trying to think our way to the finish line for every possible scenario. While the worst cases rarely come about, they affect our emotional resilience, productivity, and creativity. As a sales leader, you can't prevent all of this mental anguish, but you can significantly diminish it by being transparent and creating certainty where you can.

Create Certainty with the Three C's

Here are three tactical principles that can help you create the certainty your team craves:

1 **CONFIRM: UNCERTAINTY GROWS QUICKLY IN A VACUUM.** When your people aren't sure what information is true, false, known, or unknown, anxiety builds. Stop the emotional spiral by confirming the facts surrounding a situation, illuminating areas of doubt or uncertainty, and discouraging the sharing of misinformation. Move your team's inner dialogue from the part of the brain associated with emotion and avoidance to the part associated with logic and reason, and they'll be able to understand the path forward more clearly. For example, acquisition rumors, speculation about potential layoffs, or upcoming promotion considerations are all

instances in which confirming what might be known or unknown is helpful. Of course, this doesn't mean that all information needs to be public.

2   **COMMUNICATE: DON'T SHY AWAY FROM OPEN DIALOGUE OR TOUGH CONVERSATIONS.** When the lines of communication don't flow freely, unproductive rumors and speculation grow. Regular team meetings, written updates, informative one-on-ones, and coaching conversations (which we'll discuss in chapter 5) can all help provide your team with an outlet to voice their concerns and get your perspective. Remember, people want to know what *you* think! When you find yourself in a particularly challenging situation, create predictability and opportunities for regular updates. For example, set standing team meetings to share the latest strategic updates from your senior leadership, let your team air their concerns, and brainstorm ideas to overcome them. Give your people some of the control they feel they might be losing amid uncertain situations by providing an open platform to express themselves.

3   **CLARIFY: HELP YOUR TEAM INTERPRET THE INFORMATION.** Even after confirming the known and unknown, your team may still have feelings of fear or unease about a situation. Acknowledge their feelings and validate where those feelings are justified and where they might be reframed in the face of facts and historical trends.

Promotions and Raises: Transparency in Action

Dustin Deno is the chief revenue officer (CRO) of a venture-backed, high-growth software company. Like many leaders operating in an environment fraught with uncertainty, he needs to strike a delicate balance between two major talent and operational issues. On the one hand, his young and enthusiastic sales reps are eager to learn and secure promotions that advance their careers quickly. On the other hand, the outcome he and his leadership team (not to mention his investors) are focused on is revenue growth. That left him wondering how to give his team the certainty they crave around the progress toward their next role, while aligning everyone with the organization's revenue goals. His solution was elegant and innovative and incorporates heavy doses of powerful transparency.

First, Deno established customer segments for the sales roles needed within his team: growth, mid-market, and strategic. Next, he established three levels of proficiency within those segments based on two key metrics: the consistency of the rep's sales performance and learning. An example of what would be included in the first segment is shown in the table below.

Segment	Level 1	Level 2	Level 3
Growth Reps			
Sales Performance	Consistent quota/ target attainment for 3 months	Consistent quota/ target attainment for 3 months	Consistent quota/ target attainment for 3 months
Learning	Completion of Core training course track	Completion of Advanced training course track	Completion of Expert training course track
Mid-Market Reps			
Sales Performance			▼
Learning			▼
Strategic Reps			
Sales Performance			▼
Learning			▼

Level 1 focuses on "how to do the job," level 2 focuses on "how to master the job," and level 3 is all about "how to do the next job." The first key metric is sales performance. Sales performance for growth reps with monthly quotas who are focused on smaller, more transactional deals is determined by the rep's ability to hit their revenue targets for three months in a row (as shown in the table). Sales performance for mid-market reps with quarterly quotas who work more strategic deals with longer sales cycles is determined by the rep's ability to hit their revenue targets for two quarters is a row.

The second key metric is learning. Learning is determined at all levels by the rep's successful completion of relevant courses and exercises in their learning management system.

By codifying the required amount of knowledge, skill, and consistency required within each segment and level, Deno was able to establish promotion metrics that were transparent and certain. This virtually eliminated the unproductive mental bandwidth reps often dedicate to posturing for the next promotion. If the rep meets the objective criteria for their category and level, they are automatically promoted to the next level or segment. Not only that, but the promotion also comes with a standard increase to their on-target earnings and equity stake in the company.

Frontline sales leaders aren't left out of the mix either. For their part, managers are incentivized to ensure the majority of their team members participate in the collective attainment of the group quota. If 80 percent of their team members achieve at least 80 percent of their respective sales targets, the sales manager is allowed to hire another rep without having to take on that rep's sales quota. A huge boost for the manager! This approach also helps align leadership's objectives with the often difficult task of performance management. If a manager has a rep who isn't hitting at least 80 percent of their individual target, they are incentivized to either invest in that person's coaching and development to improve their performance or exit them from the business if they no longer believe that's possible.

Not only does this transparent framework provide team members and leaders with the certainty they need to promote focus and reduce distractions, but it also has two other benefits. First, it promotes longevity. When reps see a consistent path for learning and career growth at their company, they stay longer. Second, it provides a throttle mechanism for senior leaders to decide how quickly or conservatively they wish to grow the business. For example, by shifting the criteria for 80 percent of reps to achieve at least 80 percent of their quotas down to 70 percent for each metric, the team is able expand more rapidly. Moving the bar up to 85 or 90 percent can slow things down.

Transparency Exercise

Bringing our attention back to the fundamentals of creating transparency, let's consider how you can get your team to act with a greater sense of intent and purpose. To help you determine how to operationalize the tactics we've covered in this chapter, take out a piece of paper and draw a simple three-column chart like the one below.

Ask	What	Why
1.	1.	1.
2.	2.	2.
3.	3.	3.

In the first column, list some of the most important things you might ask your team to do—things that perhaps they don't do with the frequency and intensity they need to today. For example, these might include keeping the CRM up to date with the latest opportunity data, engaging in prospecting activities that generate pipeline, or coming to your weekly team meetings prepared to discuss the details of their sales forecast.

In the second column, list what you want your team to do—in other words, how they will fulfill the ask. This can include specific activities, metrics, the templates you'd like them to use, the outcomes you'd like them to drive, and reference examples of what *good* looks like.

In the third column, list the business insights, rationale, data points, or authentic personal perspectives you feel will help motivate them to take the action you're asking for.

Come up with a few examples and deploy them within your team in the coming days and weeks to see how invoking the simple power of transparency can have a big impact on your leadership motion and business.

3

SKILL 2

Protecting and Advocating

Medal of Honor

In the US Armed Forces, the Medal of Honor is the very highest military decoration awarded to American servicepeople. To earn it, heroes need to have distinguished themselves by committing acts of "conspicuous gallantry and intrepidity at the risk of life above and beyond the call of duty." It is also customary (and, in fact, required by the US Air Force) for members of all uniformed services to salute recipients of the Medal of Honor as a sign of respect regardless of rank or status and whether or not they are in uniform. This counts as one of the very few instances when a living member of the military can receive a salute from a higher-ranking member.

Since the Civil War, only 1,968 individuals have received this top honor. And on October 15, 2013, US Army Captain William Swenson became one of them.

On September 8, 2009, Captain Swenson's team was charged with escorting a group of government officials to a meeting with elders in the village of Ganjgal, Kunar Province, Afghanistan. As they moved through the region, they were ambushed and surrounded on three sides by over sixty enemy fighters armed with rocket-propelled grenades, mortars, and machine guns. Acting quickly, Captain Swenson returned fire, coordinated the Afghan Border Police response, and called in artillery and aviation support. As the battle wore on over the course of six grueling hours, without hesitation and ignoring the enemy's demands for his surrender, he led his team in an unarmored vehicle into the kill zone to recover wounded and missing soldiers. Exposing himself multiple times to enemy fire, he was able to administer medical aid to a wounded comrade and lob a grenade at the enemy before moving the soldier to a medevac helicopter for air evacuation. Even more remarkable than these acts of heroism, one of the medics on the helicopter had a GoPro camera on his helmet that captured Captain Swenson giving the wounded soldier a kiss on his forehead before he returned to the battlefield to rescue more. In total, he was able to recover four wounded soldiers that day.

In his popular TED talk "Why Good Leaders Make You Feel Safe," author Simon Sinek recounts Captain Swenson's incredible tale of heroism and, after seeing the video footage, admits pondering in bewilderment, "Where do people like that come from?" His first conclusion was that the military attracts altruistic individuals who are simply "better" than everyone else. In other words, their patriotic nature and larger-than-average risk tolerance draws them to a life of service. But after interviewing many such heroes, he realized his assumption was completely wrong. When he asked these people why they chose to risk their lives and commit unbelievable and selfless acts, they all said the same thing: "Because they would have done it for me."

With the right environment, leadership, and a deep sense of trust and cooperation, your team has the ability to do incredible things too!

Safety the Superpower

In his book *Leaders Eat Last*, Sinek describes a concept he calls the circle of safety. It's based on the premise that our environment is filled with forces that are out to harm or hold us back. In all cases, these environmental stressors consume our focus and serve to distract us as we try to mitigate the danger they represent.

Source: Simon Sinek, *Leaders Eat Last: Why Some Teams Pull Together and Others Don't* (New York: Portfolio/Penguin, 2017), 25.

In the very literal sense, this concept harkens back to our primitive days when we were concerned that a wild jungle animal might leap out of the darkness and ravage our village while we slept. In the corporate world, those dangers could be the economic climate, the ups and downs of the stock market, or the risk that our products and services could be rendered obsolete by advances in artificial intelligence or new technologies. In your personal life, those dangers could be disease, physical injury or insecurity, social injustice, or financial instability.

And on the sales floor, it could be poorly set quotas or targets, lack of support from your leader or organization, or fear of punitive action or termination if your goals aren't achieved.

As we've already discussed, our brains are highly evolved prediction machines. That means we're always on the lookout for potential threats and dangers in our environment and, in many cases, preemptively formulating countermeasures should those threats materialize. We save money for a "rainy day." We try our best to keep our neighborhoods safe and lock our doors at night to protect our families. We exercise, practice meditation, and take vitamins to improve our well-being. We spend time with friends and family who provide us with love and laughter. And we give ourselves emotional comfort by making up stories as to why the attractive person we met at the bar didn't call us back after our first date or why that strange dark spot we suddenly noticed on our back is "probably nothing."

Of course, some of these dangers are outside our control as individuals. For those threats, we look to others, our leaders and tribes, who we hope have made the necessary investments to secure our safety. We trusted the protectors of our ancestral communities to stand guard and keep the fires burning while we slept. We trust our armed forces to secure our borders, and we elect governments to establish socioeconomic policies that help us thrive. At home, we look to our family and friends for the love and support we need to achieve emotional balance. As children, we looked to our parents and guardians to take us where we needed to go, support us financially, and provide the necessities of life. And at work, we look to our leaders to represent our interests to the greater organization, make operational and tactical decisions that set us up for success, and provide caring guidance and coaching to help us grow personally and professionally.

But imagine for a moment what would happen if your circle of safety was absent in any of these areas. Perhaps one of your neighbors experienced a home robbery. Your retirement investment portfolio suddenly crashed. You were diagnosed with a serious disease. Or a global pandemic caused widespread supply chain disruptions and business closures, significantly impacting your ability to thrive. Fear, uncertainty, and distraction would set in. Your mind would become preoccupied with thoughts of threats and imbalance. You would spend far less time and mental energy focused on growth and more time focused on self-preservation, maintaining the status quo, and reestablishing that circle of safety. On the flip side, something amazing happens when that circle of safety is naturally present. With key fears and distractions of the outside world eliminated, we're able to focus on the task at hand, be present, and achieve incredible things.

As a sales leader, your job is to protect your team and provide them with a safe environment in which to grow and do their best work.

Fear of Forecasting

One of the most poignant examples of where creating a culture of safety can have a big impact on your sales leadership role lies in the realm of revenue forecasting. As a sales leader, your company counts on you to help predict the future by harmonizing the data in your CRM and other systems with insights from the sales floor. As we discussed in chapter 2, one of the ways you can increase the accuracy of your sales forecast is to create transparency regarding the process. In other words, help your team understand what the forecast data will be used for and how decisions are made based on it, and show them examples of what *good* forecast rigor looks like. But when it comes to subjective, emotionally driven activities like forecasting, even the most transparent sales leaders can find their effectiveness lacking if a circle of safety hasn't been established.

To frame the problem in a personal way, one of my fondest memories of when my kids were smaller was the tradition of making waffles for them on Saturday morning. While they were equally excited about this weekly ritual, they would often wake up early and head down to the kitchen to sneak in a bowl of cereal or, more often, a secret handful of chocolate chips before I got on the scene. On one such Saturday morning, I heard the kids stirring in the kitchen, and then a loud thud and the words "Uh oh!" filled the air. I arrived shortly thereafter to find a chair propped against the fridge, providing easy access to the baking supply cupboard above it. An open bag of chocolate chips was on the floor, its contents strewn about the place. And on the couch sat three guilty-looking faces. When I asked, "What happened?" the kids looked at each other, confused, as if I had asked for directions to a train station in a foreign language. They were frozen, reluctant to respond because they feared the consequences their answer might invoke.

The same thing happens to your team every time you ask your reps to submit their sales forecasts.

It's no secret that reps often tread carefully in the forecasting arena so as not to invoke any undue pipeline or performance scrutiny. If a rep's pipeline is anemic and they don't have enough deals, activities, or momentum to make their quota, they might be tempted to pad their forecast with metrics and opportunities that aren't real. On the flip side, if their pipeline is healthy and robust, with many ripe opportunities poised to close in the near term, they might still choose to downplay or "sandbag" their forecast. By intentionally lowering expectations and holding back or delaying sales, not only might they avoid undue inspection, but they also have the chance to be a hero should they over-deliver on the low bar they set.

In both instances, the fear of consequences drives the rep to misrepresent the true state of their sales performance, making the task of forecasting your business much more difficult. What's even worse is that over time these behaviors will erode the level of trust between you, your reps, and your senior leaders. This is especially problematic because, as we discussed in chapter 1, fostering these trusting relationships is absolutely critical when it comes to being the type of leader your team would fight to work with again.

Fortunately, the solution to addressing both my chocolate chip waffle disaster and the accuracy of your sales forecast is simple: establish a circle of safety. For example, when I arrived in the kitchen, consider what would have happened if I had taken the emotion out of the narrative, adopted a softer tone, and qualified my purpose with a statement like, "Don't worry. I'm not angry. I understand accidents happen. I just want to know who *might* have knocked the bag onto the floor so they can help me clean it up." Creating a safe environment would have made it less intimidating for my kids to engage and helped me get the result I was after.

In the case of your sales forecast, you can create a safe space for your reps to engage with the exercise in the most productive way by starting your request with a similar narrative. For example:

> For a number of reasons, forecasting is an important part of our business. Our marketing organization makes investment decisions based on the health of our pipeline, our finance team uses it to set budgets for headcount and compensation, and our senior leadership team uses those numbers to provide growth projections to our board of directors and investors. As you can imagine, given how many people rely on these numbers, it's important for them to be as accurate as possible. That's why my suggestion to you is to take the emotion out of the exercise. Whether your numbers are good or bad or whether you're confident or uncertain about them, the most important thing is knowing what's really going on in the business. If the numbers are great, awesome! If not, that's OK too. The more honest you are and the more insight I have, the better position I'll be in to help and support you.

The key message for both you and your team here is that running your business on painful truths is always better than making decisions based on beautiful lies.

A good way of helping your reps understand how to look at their forecast is through a simple defensibility exercise. In it, you ask the rep to imagine they've been called into your CEO's office for an impromptu sales forecast review (pretty much the best way for any rep to spend an afternoon). The CEO doesn't have any visibility or perspective into the nature of their opportunities, nor do they have time to decipher any cryptic emotional positioning or feelings around the deals. Like a lawyer questioning a witness, they just want the facts.

Now suppose the CEO picked an opportunity off the rep's forecast and asked them about it. Would the rep be able to successfully and accurately defend, using evidence, why each opportunity was forecasted the way it was? Would they be able to justify the close date, revenue, stage, and remaining steps to bring the deal in with conviction?

As before, the key here is helping the rep remove ego and false bravado from the exercise and simply communicating which opportunities they can reasonably expect to close and why. If the deals are robust and plentiful, amazing! If they've had some bad bounces and their contingency plan to make quota involves shaking the loose change out of sofa cushions, that's important to know as well. When reps feel pressure to overstate their forecast because "something" is better than nothing, no one wins. When an attorney is attempting to vigorously uphold their client's case in court, full evidential disclosure is required.

Emotional Safety and Self-Disclosure

Fostering a culture of emotional and psychological safety can be transformative when it comes to unleashing the discretionary effort of your team. That's because the support your people need won't always be something they're willing to open up about, especially when those needs are rooted in deeply private or personal issues. This is a lesson I've learned many times in my sales leadership career and one that became particularly poignant when two unlikely life stories became intertwined. The first story began in 2011 when I was diagnosed with cancer at the age of thirty-six.

When you have cancer, the only thing you want in life is to not have cancer. Not money, a new car, nailing your sales forecast, crushing your quota, or making it to President's Club. Understandably, the diagnosis consumed my focus. But one of the toughest parts of my journey was simply opening up and telling people. My inner circle knew, of course, but I was afraid to share the news publicly. It was my own private business, and the last thing I wanted was people constantly asking me if I was OK or defining me by my disease. So I kept it to myself.

Yet despite my privacy, there were people I opened up to immediately about my experience. A colleague who was caring for his father, who had been recently diagnosed with blood cancer. A young woman and mother who had recently been diagnosed with breast cancer. And an old friend from years back who had recently lost her husband to the disease. As I began to diagnose the patterns of my candor, a clear theme emerged: When I felt the other person understood what I was going through or my story was in a position to help them, opening up felt easy and natural. The environmental variables aligned to establish a circle of safety almost instantaneously.

With the grace of my incredible family and medical team, I returned to good health and came to see my diagnosis as one of my greatest blessings for the perspective it gave me—in particular regarding the emotional struggles that so many of our team members go through, whether as a result of disease, substance abuse, personal tragedy, relationship turbulence, or being a part of traditionally marginalized, persecuted, or underrepresented groups. Enter story number two.

A few years after my cancer diagnosis, I was asked to be an executive sponsor of an internal advocacy group at my company and I readily accepted. Their focus was on cultivating community and allyship for LGBTQ+ employees across the organization. There I met one of the founders of the local chapter, a young sales rep named Bari. Bari was a gay man who came from a traditional Muslim family. In a one-on-one conversation, he shared that for many years he had hidden his sexuality from his parents and colleagues out of fear for how they might react. Would they accept him? Would they see and treat him differently? He confessed that even when he had started working at our company, he had kept that part of his identity a secret for the same reason. As I listened to Bari's powerful story and the personal journey that went along with it, my mind became consumed with how my cancer diagnosis had left me feeling the same way!

But like so many others at our company, Bari went on to share that the environment of support and acceptance he found within our walls gave him the strength and courage to finally be his authentic self. He told his parents and colleagues, who were, gratefully, very supportive. And in an instant, all the extra effort and mental energy he had been expending to protect his identity vanished. The experience was transformative, and it was all catalyzed by an environment that made him feel safe.

For a leader, creating a space where people feel they won't be punished or marginalized for being themselves or sharing their ideas, questions, concerns, and mistakes is critical. In fact, a research study of nearly 300 leaders over two and half years found that teams with high degrees of psychological safety reported higher levels of performance and lower levels of interpersonal conflict. But that result isn't surprising. Consider for a moment how much of your team's mental bandwidth is spent projecting an outward persona or facade to get others to see them, their achievements, and their behaviors in a certain way. Perhaps you do the same. Now imagine how all that mental bandwidth could be harnessed and redirected to drive real progress and business results. Never underestimate the impact that fostering a culture of emotional safety can have on your team.

Creating Safety through Advocacy

As part of the leadership surveys we would regularly conduct at my companies, one of the questions the sales reps were asked to answer was whether or not they felt their manager had their back. This simple, binary question was important because it signaled the extent to which the leader was able to create a circle of safety for their people. Was the leader looking out for their team's best interests? Did they understand the personal and professional roadblocks preventing them from growing? Did they raise the issue of those barriers with key stakeholders within the organization to address them when necessary? And did they do everything they could to remove them? This is the essence of establishing safety through advocacy. When we act as advocates for our team, we build trust, strengthen those relationships, and enlarge the circle of safety that surrounds them. All of this unlocks higher levels of discretionary effort and leads to better sales performance.

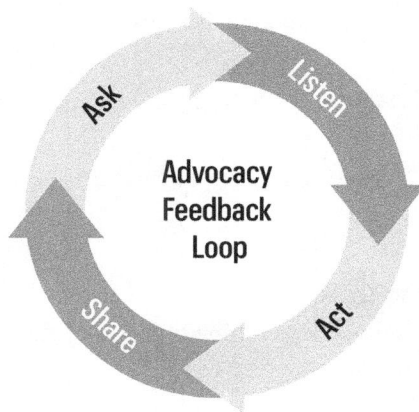

Ask

Listen

**Advocacy
Feedback
Loop**

Share

Act

Creating safety through advocacy is a simple four-step process I call the advocacy feedback loop.

Asking your team and other key stakeholders how you can best support their goals is the first step. But in many ways, asking is the easy part. Using the insights you gain to show your team you have their back, create change, and establish a circle of safety is critical to closing the advocacy feedback loop and invoking your mandate.

Ask

Step 1: Start with the Question Template

One of the easiest ways to identify the risks and barriers your reps perceive in their environment is through a simple exercise in which you ask them to complete a short sentence. I call this the One-Sentence Advocacy Builder. It's a technique adapted from one of my favorite books, *The One Thing: The Surprisingly Simple Truth behind Extraordinary Results*. In it, authors Gary Keller and Jay Papasan introduce the concept of a focusing question—an approach used to help the reader block out noise and identify the single biggest thing that might be holding them back from achieving the outcome they desire.

In the context of advocating for our sales team, the formula for this one-sentence exercise would look like this:

I could [GOAL] [TIME HORIZON] if [_____].

For example, "I could sell more products and services this quarter if..."

Step 2: Define the Goal

In the goal field, define the outcome objective your team member is driving toward. For example:

- Sell more products and services
- Build more pipeline
- Work more effectively with other departments at the company
- Expand our customer footprint in a new territory
- Increase our prospecting call rate

Although you don't always need to, you can make these outcomes more specific by including metrics. For example:

- Hit my revenue quota of $1 million in products and services
- Build a pipeline of 3× my quota coverage
- Work with marketing to generate 100 new leads
- Win ten new customers in Europe
- Make twice as many prospecting calls

Step 3: Establish the Time Horizon

In the time horizon field, set a timeframe in which the desired outcome should be achieved. For example:

- This month
- This quarter
- This year
- By a specific date
- In time for a particular season or event

Step 4: Identify the Blocker

Challenge your team member to complete the sentence with the single most impactful variable or blocker that, if addressed, would allow them to achieve the outcome.

In practice, the narrative, when used one-on-one with a sales rep, would sound something like this:

Claire, I want to make sure I'm doing everything I can to help you hit your goals this year starting with this month. So let me ask you to complete this sentence for me: "I'd stand the best chance of hitting my sales quota this month if…" What's the "if"?

Here are some examples of other one-sentence variations:

- "I could sell more products and services this quarter if…"
- "I could build more pipeline this month if…"
- "I could expand our customer footprint in Europe faster this year if…"
- "I could ramp up faster in the first thirty days of my new role if…"
- "I could close more business before the holiday season if…"
- "I could secure more revenue for our new product line next year if…"

In response to this type of question, the leaders I've worked with in my practice report hearing feedback like this:

- "…you had more time to listen to some of my customer calls and give me feedback."
- "…I was better at finding my customers' compelling events earlier in the sales cycle."
- "…my experienced teammates were more willing to share their winning secrets."
- "…I was able to strike a better work/life balance."

Running this exercise with a group of people, like your team, is an excellent way to quickly crowdsource shared feedback and blockers.

Simply replace the "I" with "we." For example, sales leaders who have asked this question in their team meetings often hear things like this:

- "... we were able to offload some of our non-selling responsibilities, like renewals, technical demos, support, and contracting, to other groups."
- "... we had a pricing model that was more competitive at the high end of the market."
- "... we updated the messaging on our website to be more consistent with the business challenges we hear from customers."
- "... we were able to respond more quickly to inbound requests for information."

Besides being one of the best and easiest ways to uncover opportunities to advocate for your team, this exercise is also one of the most powerful tools you can use in your customer discovery conversations. Depending on what you're selling, in those key initial conversations you could use the same approach and ask your customer to complete sentences like these:

- "I could deliver better patient care if..."
- "I could build a more secure network infrastructure if..."
- "I could engage more of our remote employees if..."
- "I could improve the support we provide our clients if..."
- "I could improve the conversion rate on our online store if..."

For example: "Karine, I know you mentioned delivering better business outcomes to your customers was a key focus for you. But if you had to complete this sentence for me—'I could deliver better business outcomes to my customers this year if...'—what's the 'if'?"

In my first book, *Sell the Way You Buy*, I dive deeper into the simple, science-based reason why this exercise is so engaging: people like answering questions in which they're asked to give their opinions on things. In fact, in a study conducted at Harvard University, researchers Diana Tamir and Jason Mitchell noted that 30 to 40 percent of everyday speech is used to inform others about our own subjective experiences. That means that both team members and customers are scientifically and emotionally predisposed to answering questions that require them to state their own views and opinions on a particular topic. The open-ended nature of this exercise not only ticks that box but contains the three most important elements of a good discovery question:

1 **FOCUS:** Asking a thought-provoking question and allowing the responder to select the most impactful "if" focuses them. It helps them cut out the noise and home in on the most important insights. What's that one thing that would render all the other potential options easier or unnecessary?

2 **ALIGNMENT:** By prompting the responder to discuss their needs and the support they crave, you can use that information to determine whether you can help, and if so, how. This one simple question will help you find out quickly whether or not the request is aligned with your abilities and perspectives on the problem.

3 **NOVELTY:** Fill-in-the-blank questions have an element of novelty to them. They aren't the typical discovery questions people are used to being asked. You may even get a response like "That's a really good question" when you ask it! This exercise puts the responder in a position of control, allowing them to run in any direction they like. This makes the process of revealing their problems significantly more fun than answering, "What are your problems and what support do you need?"

Maximizing Your Advocacy Impact

Here are some tips for maximizing the impact of the Ask step:

PROMOTE FOCUS: The desire to focus on the most impactful barrier to results doesn't mean there won't be multiple factors that contribute to our success or failure. The key here is coaching your team to zero in on that single biggest thing that could have the desired impact.

USE IT AS A COACHING OPPORTUNITY: Not every suggestion your team members make needs to be taken at face value. If they complete the sentence with a suggestion you don't feel makes sense, don't hesitate to challenge them on it. For example, if a team member points to the lack of a specific product feature as the reason for their low sales production, you might point out that other reps have managed to achieve their goals despite selling in the same environment. Use the exercise as an opportunity to dive deeper, ask them to consider why they've struggled where others might not have, and potentially reframe the blocker so you can better coach them through it. We'll dive deeper into this approach in chapter 5.

FOCUS ON THINGS YOU CAN CONTROL: Your rep might say they could sell more this quarter if we weren't in a recession, the Federal Reserve hadn't raised interest rates, or they hadn't just gone through a painful relationship breakup, and that might be true. It might even make sense to discuss these issues in a coaching conversation. But if these things lie outside our span of control or organizational influence, using them as the basis for this particular exercise isn't productive. In these cases, acknowledge the blocker and reframe the exercise. For example, "Shane, I completely understand that the market conditions aren't ideal for us now, but unfortunately, that's not something we can control. Setting the market conditions aside for a moment, what do you feel the number one thing holding you back from hitting your quota this quarter is?"

BE OPEN TO YOUR BLIND SPOTS: Despite your training, preparation, and desire to stay connected with your team, as a leader, you might still have blind spots. For your team, even a small change to a key process can mean the difference between sales success and failure. For example, shedding one or two low-value responsibilities, being armed with a simple one-page marketing asset to address a common objection, or even making a small change to an administrative process like travel or expense approval can have a big impact.

In other cases, your blind spots might manifest as simple misunderstandings. For example, a leader from a large enterprise software company asked his team to complete the sentence "I could sell more software this quarter if..." He was surprised when many of them came back and said "...if we could travel to meet our customers onsite more often." After all, there were no restrictions on customer-facing travel. As he dug deeper, he identified a widespread misinterpretation of a recent change to the travel policy across his team. The policy was focused on reducing discretionary travel within the company for the purposes of *internal* meetings. In fact, traveling to meet customers at their offices was highly encouraged. With the issue clarified, the blocker was instantly removed.

GO BEYOND SALES: As we discussed in chapter 1, having a strong network of relationships within our organization is a strong predictor of our revenue success as sellers and leaders. That means it's important to identify both sources of interdepartmental friction and opportunities for better collaboration with the teams we rely on to get deals done. This exercise is a perfect way to start these critical conversations.

Like loving siblings who can't seem to stop fighting in the back seat of the car on a long family road trip, one of the most strained interdepartmental relationships that exists within an organization is between sales and marketing. On the one hand, the sales team is often critical of the quality of the leads marketing passes to them. On the other hand, marketing often questions whether the sales team is working those leads as effectively as they should be. To help drive constructive dialogue between your departments, consider asking your team to complete statements like these:

- "The marketing team would be able to generate higher quality leads this year if…"

- "The one asset marketing could produce that would help accelerate sales during our new product launch is…"

- "Our website would be more effective at converting prospective buyers into leads if…"

- "We could make better use of the leads marketing sends to us this month if…"

The same approach could be used with other departments as well.

Listen

In Salesforce's 2018 *State of Sales* report, salespeople were asked to weigh in on which parts of the selling experience had an *extreme* or *substantial* impact on their ability to convert a prospect into a customer. Listening topped the list. And for good reason. In his popular TEDx talk "The Power of Listening," William Ury, co-author of the bestselling book *Getting to Yes*, summarizes the power of listening across three principles that are equally important in the realm of sales leadership:

1   **UNDERSTANDING:** To shift someone's mindset from uncertainty to safety, we need to understand the certainty they're after.

2   **CONNECTING:** Listening helps us build rapport and trust. Team members are more likely to share intimate (and more helpful) details of their challenges with us if they feel connected.

3   **RECIPROCITY:** When we listen empathetically to our team members and demonstrate a genuine interest in their feelings, they'll be more likely to listen to us when the time comes.

So after you ask your reps for their insights using the One-Sentence Advocacy Builder, here are five tips to show them you're interested and engaged.

1   **DON'T SPEAK:** This is easy to say but sometimes hard to do. You simply can't listen if you're speaking or poised on the edge of interrupting the other person. Once you ask your question, stop talking and give your reps your full attention.

2   **TAKE NOTES:** Writing things down not only helps you remember key pieces of information later on but shows your reps you're interested enough in their insights to preserve them in writing. More on this in chapter 4.

3   **USE VISUAL/AUDITORY CUES:** With the majority of our communication being non-verbal, cues like nodding and eye contact convey your focus and attention. Even in a virtual meeting or one-on-one, people can tell when you're looking at them on the screen or being distracted by something else.

4   **RECAP:** Repeating and summarizing the insights your team shared with you back to them is a great way to show them their insights have been internalized. This is especially important if the insights you sourced were in the form of a survey, a thread on your corporate communication platform, or another type of mass-collection mechanism.

5 **ASK FOLLOW-UP QUESTIONS:** Asking your team to elaborate, provide examples, or even reframe your original question is a great way
to demonstrate your genuine interest in their perspectives.

Remember, when it comes to sales leadership, just as in sales itself,
the experience is the product. Listening is one of the easiest ways you
can deepen your relationship with your team if you do it mindfully.

Act

Once you're clear on what needs to be done, it's time to get to work
on clearing those roadblocks. Showing your team you have their back
could involve streamlining your processes, investing in better tools and
technology, or facilitating collaboration with other departments. Here
are some specific examples.

Resource and Process Improvements

Much of the time, we can make life better for our reps by either simpli-
fying a complex process or providing tools or structure to keep them
on track. For example, the account executives at one of my clients
told their VP that they could close more business if they could spend
more time on their larger, more strategic opportunities. The problem
was they were getting bogged down following up on too many small-
scale leads. To fix the problem and promote focus, the VP changed the
process to allow their business development reps to qualify and close
opportunities that were less than $5,000.

Reps at another software client were struggling to establish a high-
value outbound prospecting rhythm. The hybrid workplace meant
their team wasn't always in the office at the same time. That made
sharing best-practice call scripts, narratives, and persona-targeting

strategies across the team difficult, especially for new team members. The solution was to set aside a dedicated three-hour prospecting block every Monday morning. The team would come into the office together and spend the first hour collaborating on best-practice strategies and tools for the personas they intended to target, the next thirty minutes planning the specific outreach strategies for their territory, and the final ninety minutes blitzing the phones. Not only did the strategy help boost their prospecting productivity, but the energy on the floor during these periods was palpable and reinforced the culture of effort and hustle the leader was trying so hard to foster in their hybrid work environment.

Technology Investments

The number of sales and marketing technologies available to companies is staggering, and both the volume and categories of technologies are increasing every year. For example, in 2023, companies had their choice of 11,038 marketing technologies, more than double the number available just six years prior. My advice is to be judicious with your investments. After all, tech stacks can quickly become bloated and expensive, and many platforms include a great deal of functional overlap. However, one can't deny that sometimes the right technology can be highly effective when it comes to unleashing the potential of your team.

The Gift of Time

Sometimes the greatest gift you can give your team is time. Time to not only work on deals and engage in focused work, but also to prepare, build, and simply reflect. As you saw during the focus exercise in chapter 1, many sales leaders report wanting to spend less time on low-value activities and meetings and more time on strategic activities that give them leverage. Your team is no different. One of the ways you can show them you care is to help them manage their schedules and reduce distractions. You can do this by canceling or shortening meetings to give them back time in their day. Or you can even set "disruption-free" times during the week where you turn off all notifications and emails and engage in focused work.

One of the best examples of how sales leaders can give their team the gift of time came while I was sitting at my desk back at Salesforce next to my boss, Dan Ross. Dan was the SVP of small business sales for the United States, and I was the VP who ran his business for the eastern region. I was responsible for seventy reps across three offices, and both of us always had a lot on our plates. Our downtown office was situated on the shore of Lake Ontario, close to a ferry dock that routinely shuttled tourists and locals to the Toronto Island Park, a beautiful green space where people would come to enjoy the peaceful outdoors. Between the grind of meetings and calls, Dan and I would often spend a few moments gazing out the window. Taking in the lake views during work hours was strangely calming, as was living vicariously through the people we watched cruise around it.

On one such occasion, we were looking out at the water when I casually said, "I always love going to the island with my family. But every now and then I think about just hopping on a ferry and spending the day there alone. You know. Just to be by myself, enjoy the fresh air, and get some good thinking done." Dan briefly raised his eyebrows in agreement but didn't say anything as we both quietly returned to work, burying our heads in our laptops. Moments later, an all-day calendar invite hit my inbox for the following week. It was from Dan. The title of the meeting was "Priemer's day on the island." A smile came to my face as a sense of gratitude washed over me. Never underestimate how powerful giving your team the gift of time can be when it comes to winning their hearts and minds. With just a few keystrokes, Dan showed me that day.

Departmental Representation

In some cases, the things your team needs you to fight for may not be within your control. This is where your strategy needs to shift from problem-solving and delivery to representing their interests to key outside stakeholders who can help. Whether it's requesting additional resources, budget allocation, or operational support, be their voice to ensure they have the necessary tools and support to excel. For example, your reps might tell you they'd be able to win more consistently against a pesky competitor by having a few case studies and testimonials in their back pocket from customers who recently chose your solution over theirs. In that case, you might engage your marketing department to help create the necessary assets.

In one of my former roles as VP of sales, my team was struggling with contracting support. We were selling to large enterprise customers, and their legal and procurement specialists would often request changes to the terms in our master service agreement. The problem was, we were using outside legal counsel to assist in qualifying and reframing those requests, and all that back-and-forth ended up adding days to our sales cycles. After digging deeper to understand the true impact of the need, I raised the issue and made the case to our CEO. A short time later we secured a fractional in-house counsel to ease the burden on my team and increase our deal velocity.

Opportunities for Growth

As we saw back in chapter 1 during the "best sales leader you ever had" exercise, one of the most powerful ways you can advocate for your team is by providing them with opportunities for professional development and advancement. This could include things like access to training programs, conferences, and mentorship initiatives. It can also include creating new roles within your organization and simply giving individuals a forum to step up and showcase their strengths through special projects and initiatives.

One of the key inflection points of my career was working for an amazing leader at Salesforce named Tony Rodoni, who wrote the foreword to this book. Tony ran a 600-person North American commercial sales organization, and a few years into my tenure at the company he helped create a unique evangelism role for me. The role provided an incredible platform for me to create content, pursue speaking opportunities, and produce both internal and customer-facing programs to help grow our people and business in new ways. My content started to get traction in respected publications like *Forbes* and *Entrepreneur*, and the experience fanned the flames of my passion for modern sales education. In many ways, the opportunity Tony provided for me was the catalyst for the training practice I run today and the book you're reading.

Remember, asking and listening are nothing without clearly demonstrating your commitment to your team's well-being by taking action. Make clearing their roadblocks a priority.

Share

The final step in closing the loop is maintaining an open line of ongoing communication with your team about your advocacy initiatives. This involves keeping them informed about company updates, changes in sales strategies, and any relevant information that affects their work. The frequency with which you provide these updates depends on the degree of uncertainty or emotional urgency of the situation being advocated for.

For example, at the height of the COVID-19 pandemic, when the need for timely information was in the interest of both the public and private sectors, we saw politicians, public health officials, and corporate leaders providing daily updates. In the same way, your team or

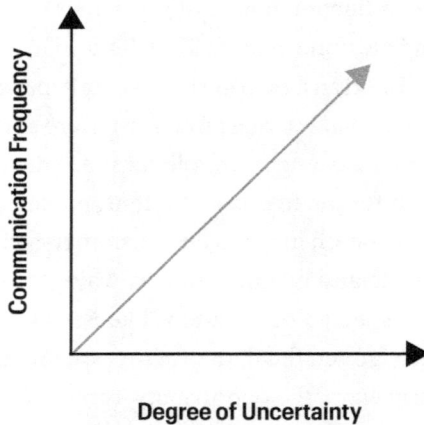

Degree of Uncertainty

rep might be working through an emotionally charged period, such as an acquisition, downsizing, new product launch, or high-pressure quarter-end revenue push. In these instances, a more frequent communication cadence with as much transparency as appropriate can be helpful.

Linking Advocacy to Results

Advocating for your reps and paving the way for their success shouldn't be a one-sided affair. Your investment of emotional, political, and financial capital, while made out of a sense of altruism, should produce results. For example, you may have modified a policy or procedure to free up more of your team's time for selling. You may have invested in new sales technologies to accelerate or automate a process. Or you may have advocated to remove a key roadblock that was causing undue distraction or frustration. Either way, it's reasonable to assume you should see a positive change in a key metric, whether it be related to revenue, retention, or growth. That's why it's important for the communication updates back to your team and key stakeholders to include details of the progress you've made.

Sharing relevant progress and results can also help address and frame future requests for support. For example, during my initial recruiting efforts after joining Salesforce, I learned that the organization had a requirement for all new sales hires to have a university-level education. Of course, one could argue that to be successful in sales you don't need to be university educated. And statistically speaking, maintaining that requirement reduced the available pool of sales rep candidates, making it harder to fill open positions. Senior leaders periodically advocated on behalf of their hiring managers to have that requirement relaxed. But many of those leaders didn't realize that when that condition had been relaxed in the past, the company had measured the effectiveness and tenure of the reps who were eventually hired and found it to be markedly lower than for their university-educated counterparts. Regardless of whether you feel you would take the same position, the results-based feedback loop was effective in informing future efforts. Yours should be too.

Recognizing Winning Behaviors

Advocating and clearing roadblocks for your team should ultimately produce positive behavior changes. As an example, let's revisit the goal statements we came up with during the first part of the One-Sentence Advocacy Builder exercise:

- Sell more products and services
- Build more pipeline
- Work more effectively with other departments at the company
- Expand our customer footprint in a new territory
- Increase our prospecting call rate

If your advocacy efforts were indeed successful in driving these outcomes, one of the keys to propagating the winning behaviors that gave rise to them is to make them visible. That means ensuring you have a mechanism to call these behaviors out when they happen—for example, sharing them on an internal social network like Slack (even with a dedicated channel) or at regular company or team meetings to drive the positive reinforcement you're after. But be careful. Superlatives like "Great job!" or "Amazing work!" aren't helpful. As we'll explore further in chapter 6, when closing the feedback loop it's important to call out and link the specific behaviors and the outcomes they drove. The more specific you can be about what was done, how, and its value in your business, the easier it will be for others to replicate the behavior.

For example, the reps at one of my software clients were struggling to convert sales leads and traced the issue back to their introductory presentations. The existing format led with product highlights, features, and benefits, which left their prospects bored and disengaged, and resulted in too many lost opportunities. Together we worked on a new format that put the changing industry landscape and the problems their prospects were experiencing front and center in the narrative. As the reps deployed the updated narrative and its positive impact on customer conversion quickly began to show, the leadership team made sure to call out the specific instances in which the new tactics had been deployed and had the reps share their success stories with the greater team.

For example, in one team's update, their VP wrote, "Excellent job Maya on your prospect presentation this morning! I loved that you got more than 75 percent of the way through the discussion before even mentioning our solutions. This made the customer super engaged and willing to share more about the problems they were experiencing. Not only that, but by focusing on their problems and not our product, your tone was much more confident and persuasive. No surprise that the customer was excited to bring their executive team onto a follow-up call with us next week. Keep it up!" The public, positive reinforcement ensured the desired behaviors continued.

Safety and Advocacy Assessment

As we close out this chapter, let's bring our attention back to the key elements required to provide teams with a blanket of safety, protection, and advocacy. Consider how you can show your team you have their back and reinforce the positive outcomes those efforts drive with this simple, three-question self-assessment:

1   What's one area of your operation where creating a culture of emotional safety can help reduce the personal or operational stress on your team, produce better results, or unlock more of their discretionary effort?

2   What's one way you can deploy the One-Sentence Advocacy Builder with your team to understand what's holding them back from doing their best work and help clear the path for them to do it?

3   What's one way you'll promote the positive behaviors and results that come from those efforts to close the loop with your team and reinforce the value of the culture of protection and advocacy you've built?

Finally, it's important to recognize that even though these exercises focus on singular actions, the process of creating a culture of emotional protection and advocacy is not a project that begins and ends, but rather an ongoing cycle. Like other positive habits, from healthy eating to exercise to self-care, as a sales leader you will get the most value from having your team's back by treating it like your full-time job. Because it is!

4

SKILL 3

Driving Accountability

Preparing for the Board Meeting

Today's the day that's been consuming your thoughts for a long time. As a sales leader, you've been asked to present a quarterly digest of your revenue performance to your company's board of directors. As you stand outside the boardroom dressed a little nicer than usual, you glimpse a collective of senior executives in expensive suits seated inside around a pristine table. Its surface reflects the bright lights from the ceiling and serves as a reminder of the polite but stern interrogation they directed at you in this very spot last time. With every quarter comes a different narrative, story, and set of explanations, and you know that today the board is eagerly awaiting yours. When you enter the room, their gazes turn to you, and even though some of them manage to crack a smile, their expressions are discerning and expectant. After all, this is a critical juncture in your company's growth, and there's little room for a missed step or target. The air of anticipation is palpable and the weight of responsibility on your shoulders is heavy. Judgment day has arrived.

For a senior sales leader, being asked to present a quarterly digest of your team's performance to your company's board of directors or senior executives comes with all the stress, anxiety, and carefully orchestrated execution of being called to testify in front of Congress. It's not surprising that many of the leaders I work with in my practice dedicate a significant amount of time to ensuring they bring a high level of focus, attention, and preparation to the task. I was no different, and you likely aren't either. It's not that the assignment itself is exceptionally difficult or that the information and data needed to support your narrative is hard to get. The pressure comes from the feelings of judgment, insecurity, and accountability not only to deliver on the board's performance expectations but also to convey a deep sense of mastery and understanding of your operation.

Whether you hit your goals or not, being armed with the insights and poise to explain why, respond to tough questions, and articulate a plan to elevate your team's performance inspires confidence. When you nail the narrative, you're seen as strong, capable, and worthy. When you don't have answers, can't defend your strategy, and don't have a plan for learning, iterating, or executing, you seem feeble and weak.

Despite how unpleasant the experience might seem, I always wished more of my reps understood what that level of accountability feels like. If they did, getting them to do things like update the CRM, try a little harder to hit their weekly activity targets, or suggest new, constructive ways to improve our operation might not seem like such a chore. Not because accountability should be ominous or invoke the specter of punitive consequences, but because it's a mechanism to encourage people to do the things they agreed to do in the first place—things that are in their best interest and help promote the growth and success of themselves and those around them.

Positive Pressure

Accountability often comes with a sense of pressure. But the pressure to live up to the commitments we make to ourselves and the stakeholders that depend on us isn't a negative thing. In fact, pressure can be both helpful and necessary. For example, in democratic societies, periodic elections help hold leaders accountable for achieving the results they promised during their campaigns. Alcoholics Anonymous helps people hold themselves accountable for their abstinence-based recovery from alcoholism. And when I chose to assume the role of a sales leader, I understood (as I hope you do too) that a certain level of accountability comes with the role.

Fortunately, most of us have nothing but positive intentions when it comes to doing the things we say we're going to do. That's why we appreciate having mechanisms in place to remind us of them. For example, if I agree to wake up early to take my daughter to her volleyball practice because I care about supporting her and her athletic pursuits, I won't object if she sends me a reminder to set an alarm the night before. This can be particularly helpful if I'm the type of person who takes a bit longer to get going in the morning. By the same token, suppose you were coaching one of your sales reps and they agreed that in order for them to hit their quota, they would need to make fifteen prospecting calls per day. If they believe you are acting in their best interest, you were transparent about why you chose that number, and you've created a sense of mutual alignment, they will see the layer of accountability you've provided for the task as collaborative and welcome. This would be especially true if they're someone who admits they're prone to distraction.

Former college president David Bednar told a story in his general conference about the simple power of positive pressure. A young man drove his pickup truck into the snowy mountains, and as the snow fell, the rear wheels of the truck struggled to gain traction. Finally, unable to move, the man became stranded. After some frustration, he was at last able to free himself by filling the bed of the truck with wood. Its weight and pressure created the traction the man needed. Similarly, the positive pressure created by a sense of accountability can be very productive and, in many cases, necessary.

There are many ways sales leaders can inspire greater levels of rep accountability. Unfortunately, over the years I've also seen too many try to administer it the wrong way.

At some point in your sales career, you've likely crossed paths with a heavy-handed leader who publicly berated and embarrassed reps on forecast calls or in business review meetings. Whether it was their poor quota attainment, low level of effort or activity, or an unexplained series of competitive losses, their perceived lack of productivity and preparedness was met with a decidedly aggressive response. Over time, many salespeople develop a thick skin as a result of the constant rejection they need to endure. And while a natural tolerance of rejection from customers and prospects is one thing, experiencing public shaming from a sales leader rarely produces the desired level of motivation. Even worse, the behavior can foster a toxic work environment and absolutely eviscerate a productive and trusting relationship almost instantaneously.

> "I was talking to a group of CEOs recently when one of them told a story," said Don Rheem, CEO of Washington, DC–based E3 Solutions and author of *Thrive by Design: The Neuroscience That Drives High-Performance Cultures* ... "He said, 'Yesterday I got furious with one of my senior leaders because of a mistake he made. I ripped into him during our senior leadership meeting. I was so convinced the problem we were having was all his fault. And then I was sitting at my home computer when I received a notification from LinkedIn that Bob had just updated his profile, and my heart sank as I realized he might be about to quit.'"

If you found yourself in the same position as that CEO, would you stand behind your behavior, or would you find yourself immediately regretting it?

Numerous research studies illustrate why berating or embarrassing employees at work is bad for both the individual and the organization. For example, a study published in the *Journal of Occupational Health Psychology* found that employees who experienced workplace incivility, such as being berated or embarrassed in front of others, reported higher levels of psychological distress and lower levels of job satisfaction and organizational commitment. A study published in the *Journal of Business Ethics* found that employees who experienced abusive supervision, such as being yelled at or belittled by their supervisor, were more likely to engage in counterproductive work behaviors, such as intentionally wasting time or resources. And a study published in the *Academy of Management Journal* found that employees who experienced abusive supervision had higher levels of stress and lower levels of job performance, which ultimately led to lower levels of customer satisfaction.

These studies illustrate that these behaviors are not only morally wrong but also counterproductive for organizations, leading to reduced job satisfaction, increased turnover, and decreased revenue productivity.

So how can sales leaders drive higher levels of accountability within their organizations? Here are five powerful ways that will not only help your team be more productive but actually strengthen the relationship between you and each other:

1   Write things down.
2   Let the data do the hard work.
3   Show them what "good" looks like.
4   Promote ongoing practice.
5   Deputize your team.

Let's look at them one by one.

Write Things Down

It's funny how sometimes the most powerful productivity and account-ability hacks are also the easiest. This became clear to me when I was building and leading the sales team at my third startup. The company was called Rypple, and our solution was a software platform that helped employees get the feedback, coaching, and recognition they craved at work. It was based on the premise that, in a world driven by social media, people (in particular the millennials who were flooding the workforce at the time) love getting real-time insights into how they are doing in their jobs. They also hate having to wait for their annual performance reviews to get it. Our company ended up being acquired by software giant Salesforce (which is how I came to work there), and the product was eventually integrated into their platform as a tool to drive better sales performance.

One of the key underlying premises of the solution was this: whether you're talking about a once-a-year review or even a weekly one-on-one coaching session, all of the critical events related to a rep's performance happen between those checkpoints. Those include things like goals, deadlines, key performance indicators, strategic delivera-bles, team commitments, day-to-day tasks, and even good deeds. The problem is that unless we find a way to track and memorialize these things, they often go unnoticed, unmanaged, and forgotten. Unfortu-nately, maintaining an encyclopedic memory of all of them is neither practical nor possible. David Allen, management consultant, author, and founder of the famous "Getting Things Done" movement, says, "Your mind is for having ideas, not holding them." But when we let the commitments we make to ourselves, our leaders, and our teams fall off the radar, revenue growth, career progress, and fostering trust become much more difficult.

The good news is that driving accountability by writing things down doesn't have to be time-consuming or complicated. Here are a few tips to help you figure out where and how to do it.

WHERE:

1 **ENSURE MUTUAL ACCESSIBILITY:** You might be tempted to scribble some notes down in your trusty notebook, phone, or tablet, or log them in your calendar to jog your memory later on. But those are poor choices unless the other person (or people) you're trying to hold accountable has access to the same information. Regardless of where you keep track of things, make sure everyone who needs to see it can.

2 **AVOID EMAIL, TEXT, OR MESSAGING APPS:** Despite being digital and easy to access, thread-based messaging systems have a bad habit of losing details, especially when more than one other party is involved. Besides their being notoriously difficult and time-consuming to search, a conversation's key information can be easily pushed up and out over time.

3 **KEEP SECURE AND IDEALLY AUDITED:** Since the things you might be discussing are sensitive or relevant to a specific individual or group, make sure you have the ability to securely control access to them. Additionally, having an audit trail can prevent key information from accidentally or intentionally being changed.

In most cases, something simple and generally free, like a Google Doc or spreadsheet, can tick all these boxes. And to the extent that the platform can be easily accessed via a mobile device, even better!

HOW:

1   **SHARE THE RESPONSIBILITY:** Just because you're the one tasked with driving the accountability doesn't mean you always need to be the one to write things down. In fact, asking the other person (or a designated individual in the case of a group) to document or update the content has three big benefits. First, it makes life easier for you. Second, it engages others in the process, increasing their level of commitment to it. And third, it helps validate whether they are aligned in their understanding of the instructions, next steps, and deliverables you discussed.

2   **MAKE IT AN ONGOING PROCESS:** Driving accountability by writing things down doesn't have to be something you only do after a meeting or event. Turning instructions, to-do lists, and coaching advice into living, breathing artifacts that can be modified and updated on the fly is not only helpful but encouraged. After all, in the modern, hybrid work environment, inspiration and updates can happen anytime.

3   **LESS IS OFTEN MORE:** Don't worry about writing every last insight, instruction, or piece of advice down. Simply focus on the important things you'd like to remember and promote accountability for. For example, suppose you were onboarding a new rep to your team. There might be certain activities or milestones you would want them to hit in their first month. By keeping that list short and tight, you would not only help promote accountability but also focus on that critical initial period. If everything is important, nothing is.

Noorelle Sullivan is a sales manager at a fast-growing software company and one of the leaders I coach in my practice. Her team loves her because she demonstrates a genuine sense of caring and is always looking for ways to help them improve their game. As with many sales

teams, her team's customer calls are recorded. That's especially helpful because when Noorelle makes a suggestion or introduces a new
tactic as part of the coaching she provides, she'll often ask the reps to
come to their next meeting with a recorded example of how they used
the tactic in the field. The problem is, despite their best intentions,
they weren't always remembering to do that. "Oh shoot! I'm sorry, I
totally forgot to bring a call sample" was a common refrain. To help
keep the ask top of mind, Noorelle started creating a simple reminder
in the online tool her company provides to support her coaching. Not
only did it help her reps come to their sessions more prepared, but also
their performance improved as a result.

But her focus on writing things down isn't restricted to one-on-
ones. She encourages her team to take the same approach to driving
self-accountability in all their customer interactions. For example,
before getting on a customer call, her team writes their goals for the
conversation down to ensure they maintain focus and achieve them
by the end. Any key data points or information needed to move the
opportunity along are also highlighted to ensure they're not missed.

Let the Data Do the Hard Work

Walking into a meeting with your manager, senior executives, or
board of directors is always easier (and more fun) when you've been
crushing your sales numbers. After all, most of us prefer high-fives,
congratulations, and fewer questions to judgment, pipeline inspection, and awkward conversations. The same goes for your team. But
since even the best reps spend the majority of the selling period behind
their targets than ahead of them, driving accountability in your regular conversations with them can feel uncomfortable. And when things
feel uncomfortable, whether it's exercise, healthy eating, or pulling

out of a dead-end relationship, we tend to avoid them despite their importance.

But reviewing activity and pipeline metrics during your one-on-one or team meetings is both time-consuming and unnecessary. After all, your meeting shouldn't be like a reality show results episode. In a world where most sales teams track their activity, pipeline, and revenue metrics in their CRM or sales engagement platform, there should be no surprises as to where your team stands. That means both parties should have access to any data (contentious or otherwise) you plan to discuss and come to the conversation already having reviewed it. That way you can take the emotion out of the experience and instead focus on root causes and action items.

Here are four simple steps for letting the data do the hard work for you.

Step 1: Identify the Desired Behaviors

Before you get into the metrics themselves, start by deciding *which* behaviors you'd like to see more of. For example, if prospecting is important for your business, you might be trying to get your team to make more cold calls. However, simply making a certain number of dials may not be enough to achieve the results you're looking for. Instead, you'd want to focus on getting the prospect to actually pick up the phone and engage. To do that, you might need to have them make calls during a certain time of day or to a specific type of customer based on their industry, company size, or job title.

Imagine your reps can sell products and services to both new and existing customers. Since selling into the existing customer base is easier than pursuing new clients, your reps may bias toward that motion even though it won't be sufficient to drive the revenue growth your company expects. That means you'll need to focus the accountability exercise on driving new-client-acquisition behaviors.

Or perhaps your company sells multiple products and services and just introduced a brand new offering. In order to hit your growth targets, you need to get your reps to sell more of that new solution even though it's unfamiliar and less comfortable for them to position with customers.

Step 2: Decide Which Metrics to Track

Once you've settled on the behaviors you're trying to drive, you'll need to figure out which metrics provide an accurate picture of whether your reps are engaging or being successful in those behaviors. Keep in mind that metrics can take many forms. Some helpful statistics are readily available for reporting in your CRM and other revenue systems, while others can be computed using these foundational data points, often in the same systems. For example, core sales statistics like the number of calls and emails a rep initiates, pipeline amount by sales stage and lead source, closed revenue, lost opportunities, average deal size, and sales cycle length can be easily reported on. But suppose you have a rep who struggles with forecast accuracy because their deals keep slipping as the quota period draws to a close. You might choose to calculate a "push counter" metric. Here, each time the rep pushes a deal out beyond the period for which it was originally forecasted, the counter increments by one. The goal in coaching that rep would be to reduce their push counter over time.

Or perhaps your goal is to have your reps reach out to all new leads generated by the marketing or sales development team within the first hour after they come in to maximize the conversion opportunity. Here you might choose to calculate a "time to first touch" metric and work with your team to minimize that time. In fact, a study that analyzed three years' worth of data, 100,000 call attempts, six companies, and 15,000 leads showed a 400 percent decrease in odds of qualifying leads when reps waited ten minutes or more to follow up.

One of my favorite reports to run as VP of sales was called "stage-to-dead," and it helped answer an important question about deals we ended up losing: "What stage of the sales cycle was the deal at before we lost it?" For example, are we losing deals efficiently, during the discovery phase, before we invest too much time? Or are they being lost later on, such as during the procurement or negotiation process? A consistent trend toward the latter could point to a possible broken pricing model or new competitive threat. If the trend is isolated to a single rep, the pattern of moving deals through the funnel hastily or without proper scrutiny could be caused by a fear of not showing enough traction in their territory.

Step 3: Choose Where to Display the Metrics

Most systems in your sales technology stack will have reports, dashboards, notifications, and the ability to integrate both with one another and with other communication tools within your company. That means you'll have lots of options as to where and how to display that data. For example, across my leadership roles I used a series of reports and dashboards that served different purposes and, as such, had different delivery mechanisms.

Singular reports were used to show things like opportunities generated by the business development team that had yet to be touched by a rep, or close rates by rep by customer industry. Additionally, we had other dashboards that served specific functions, each with several report widgets. One dashboard was focused on the progress toward our monthly goals and included details related to sales rep activity like emails, phone calls, pipeline generation, deal progression, and closed business. Another dashboard was focused on sales pipeline and included details related to opportunities by lead source, product mix, and whether the opportunity was with a new or existing customer. You should combine your data into a format and medium that makes the most sense for your business and the behaviors you're trying to drive.

For example, you might combine a variety of report widgets that are especially useful in the one-on-one coaching sessions with your reps into a single dashboard.

Step 4: Define the Use Case

Finally, you should be clear on when these reports, dashboards, and other proactive alerts should be used. For example, the report showing opportunities generated by the business development team that had yet to be touched might be delivered to everyone on your team via email once a week. On the other hand, reps might be given instructions to review the dashboard that illustrates the progress toward their monthly goals before each one-on-one meeting with their manager and come prepared to discuss the data and insights it conveys. A different dashboard might be used in preparation for your quarterly business review meetings. Real-time alerts in your corporate communication tool can be used to notify team members of wins. Still others might simply be static reports, accessed on demand when needed.

The trick to making the data do the hard work for you is ensuring it's both accessible and visible. Unless the data is particularly sensitive, it's recommended that the whole team, business unit, or even company be able to see it. Data is cold and impartial. It has no feelings and bears no intent, and its meaning is only assigned by those who view it. Those who find themselves positioned favorably in these reports, dashboards, and alerts should have something to celebrate. To those who find themselves falling behind, you might suggest they arrive at the conversation accountable and prepared to discuss their ideas on how to get things trending in the right direction.

To help crystalize this approach, draw a simple chart like the one to follow. Then consider at least three behaviors you'd like to drive within your team and the associated metrics, location, and use case for each before continuing. I've put an example in the first column.

	1.	**2.**	**3.**
Behavior	Reduce number of stale opportunities in sales pipeline to ensure forecasts are accurate		
Metrics	Opportunities open >120 days with out-of-date next steps (typical sales cycle is <90 days)		
Location	"Opportunities Requiring Attention" dashboard in CRM system		
Use Case	Dashboard can be viewed/refreshed on demand in CRM system and delivered via email to the team every Monday at 9 AM		

Show Them What "Good" Looks Like

In chapter 2 we discussed the power of showing your team what good looks like in the context of creating transparency. There I gave two different examples where we sent our sales reps into the field to deliver news of a potentially contentious pricing change to our customers.

In the first instance, we didn't provide any details about how the task should be done or how we expected the narrative to sound. As a result, we ended up running into trouble when our team was left to figure it out on their own and improvise. As a leadership team, one could argue that we had the right to be upset and disappointed. After all, the task seemed straightforward, and it was the sales reps who failed to communicate the news of the price change in the most effective way. But how could we be disappointed or hold them accountable when we never showed them what "good" looked or sounded like in the first place? That's why, in the second instance, we were much more prescriptive about how the task was to be executed. By providing a gold standard for the behavior, we helped set our team up for success and built trust along the way by doing it. But that standard also established a framework to hold the team accountable for the outcome.

To be clear, engaging in the practice of setting standards doesn't mean that, as a leader, you'll get it right all the time. You probably have memories of leaders asking you to do things in a way that didn't make sense or align with your personal philosophy. In fact, by coloring outside the lines of the prescribed standard, you and your teammates may have even achieved a better result. As leaders, it's important to be open to feedback, especially in the area of process improvement (a topic we'll be discussing later). But accountability cannot exist in the absence of standards.

It also doesn't imply that every task or action in your team's repertoire needs to have a standard. For example, you don't need to tell your reps not to use inappropriate language in their customer emails or show up to key executive meetings wearing sweatpants. But when it comes to more specific tasks, especially for reps who might be new to your company, industry, or even the role itself, setting standards of performance and execution can be extremely important, like these:

- What does a good product pitch sound like?
- What does an accurate sales forecast look like?
- How quickly do we expect a new rep to ramp up and hit their quota?
- How do the best reps at our company handle price objections?
- What does a properly executed executive meeting or customer event look like?

In each instance, if you want to hold your team accountable for the outcome, it's important to ensure the standard is clear, visible, and easily accessible. For example, I work with many of my clients on revamping their corporate pitches and introductory sales presentations. Once we've refined the narrative and content, we get a senior member of the sales or leadership team to deliver it while they're being recorded. The recording is then posted to a central location and baked into the new hire onboarding process.

So if you're frustrated or concerned about your team's lack of consistency or progress when it comes to how they execute a specific task or process, ask yourself if you've set a clear and visible standard for what good looks like. If not, the accountability for their success may sit solely on you.

Promote Ongoing Practice

In 1976, 15 percent of American adults were obese. In 2020, that number skyrocketed to almost 42 percent. Do these statistics point to a decline in the amount of information and standards available about how to maintain a healthy lifestyle through diet and exercise? Unlikely. In their book *The Knowing-Doing Gap*, Stanford University business professors Jeffrey Pfeffer and Robert Sutton apply a similar lens to the world of leadership. In it, they ask, "Did you ever wonder why so much education and training, management consultation, organizational research, and so many books and articles produce so few changes in actual management practice?" The reason is the same in both instances.

Across many practices and competencies, there is a difference between concepts we are able to understand and those we can successfully execute with a degree of mastery and consistency. Sales is no different. It's simply not enough to point to a list of resources and standards, say, "Do it that way!" and expect results. It's the responsibility of a leader to drive accountability for ongoing practice and reinforcement if they want to improve the performance of their team.

Fortunately, there are some simple ways you can promote ongoing practice of the tactics you want to drive accountability for.

"What Are You Doing Differently?"

In this approach, you use the first five or ten minutes of your regular team meetings to have team members share updates or changes they've made to their sales motions over the past week based on any new knowledge, training, or processes they've incorporated.

There are two ways to do this. The first way is simply asking team members to volunteer their insight as part of the exercise, similar to a teacher calling students to the front of the class to share their homework from the day before. For example, you might say, "A couple of weeks ago we shared a helpful customer-facing narrative to position the upcoming price increase. Who would like to share how they've used this in the field and what the customer's response was?"

The key to making this work is setting expectations. The team should be told in advance that you'll be soliciting their insights so the exercise doesn't come as a surprise. While you won't have time for everyone to share, they should know you'll be calling on a few of them at random. The fair warning combined with the social pressure associated with not wanting to seem unprepared in front of their peers provides the motivation and accountability to practice the tactic ahead of time, which is your ultimate goal.

The second way involves hand-selecting individuals to provide their insights in advance of your team meeting based on the behaviors you observed in the field. For example, during your coaching, call reviews, or meeting ride-alongs, you may have noticed a rep handling a customer objection about a new price increase with masterful precision. In that instance, you might say something like, "I really liked the way you handled the objection about the price increase back there. You clearly laid out the reason and timing for the change, and your tone was humble and empathetic. At our next team meeting, would you be up for sharing your story and approach with everyone? I think they'd get a ton of value from it." This action has two big benefits. First, your praise makes your team member feel good! Second, reinforcing a specific winning behavior as it happens helps crystalize it for the rep, making it more likely they'll repeat it in the future. And in case you're wondering, yes, harkening back to what we discussed earlier in this chapter, writing down the tactical narrative and the reminder to share it will help keep both things top of mind.

Stand and Deliver

This simple approach is highly effective when it comes to certifying that your team is able to execute a specific narrative, presentation or demonstration script, or tactic. After providing the required content, instructions, and ideally a standard for what good looks like, schedule time for the person to stand in front of you, their colleagues, or a panel of your choosing and deliver it as though they're doing it in front of a customer. A single leader or a smaller group represents a lesser collective bandwidth commitment. However, depending on the nature and duration of the task, getting feedback from a larger audience can not only be valuable but also create a shared "rite of passage" experience within your team.

To promote consistency in how you evaluate your team's performance using this exercise and provide them with specific feedback on how to improve it, it can be helpful to have a rubric to score them against. For example, one dimension of your team's ability to deliver content might be their ability to integrate relevant and powerful customer stories into their narrative. A four-level grading system for that skill might look something like this:

- **LEVEL 1**: Rep fails to effectively integrate customer stories to support key points or fails to connect them to the audience's needs and pain points.

- **LEVEL 2**: Rep attempts to integrate customer stories but lacks effectiveness in supporting key points or connecting with the audience's needs and pain points.

- **LEVEL 3**: Rep effectively leverages customer stories to support key points and connects them to the audience's needs and pain points, enhancing the overall impact of the presentation.

- **LEVEL 4**: Rep skillfully integrates a variety of customer stories to create a compelling narrative that powerfully supports key points and resonates with the audience, leaving a lasting impression through impactful storytelling.

The same approach can be applied to other dimensions, such as the rep's knowledge of market, ability to recall and incorporate key solution messages and features, use of natural and authentic language, and fluidity of their delivery.

Group Call Review

This powerful approach is one I use consistently in my training and coaching practice. While it might seem scary or intimidating for your team at first, it's one of the highest-value and most motivating activities you can do with your reps. Unlike the first two, this approach doesn't involve your team members sharing any stories, lessons learned, or situational role-play. Instead, it has the group reviewing actual audio or video meeting footage of their colleagues deploying specific tactics or narratives with customers in the field and providing feedback.

Once you've conducted the training, provided the necessary support materials, and showcased examples of what good looks like to your team, it's a simple three-step process:

1 **SELECT THE TACTIC(S):** Identify the specific tactics or narratives you're looking to reinforce with your team. If you've recently covered a variety of them, it's best to keep the scope for this exercise narrow, focusing on a single narrative or a few tactics at a time. For example, if your team has recently been struggling to deal with a recurring price objection, a pitch surrounding a new product release, or a negotiation tactic regarding discount requests, focus on that.

2 **REQUEST EXAMPLES:** Ask that reps return to the group in a set time-frame, for example at the next team meeting, with a call recording or video meeting snippet from real customer interactions where the tactic was used, and that they be prepared to share them. Conversational analytics tools and sales engagement platforms like Gong, Chorus, Outreach, and Salesloft make this very easy to do. In fact, most of them can be programmed to identify portions of a conversation where specific words and phrases are used. The samples should include only 30 to 120 seconds of footage relevant to the tactic you're practicing, not the entire conversation. If collecting live samples isn't possible for security or privacy reasons, first-hand stories can be substituted.

3 **SHOW AND TELL:** When the reps return to a group setting, remind everyone of the task, provide transparency about why the behaviors are important, and call on them to share their recording of the customer interaction with the group one by one. Prior to reviewing the

call, the rep should be instructed to provide context for the interaction everyone is about to hear with the group. I often liken this to a movie star setting up a clip of their latest film with a late-night talk show host. Once the clip has been shared, as the leader, you'll likely have specific thoughts and feedback on what you feel the rep did well and where you feel they can improve. However, I recommend you encourage the team to provide their thoughts to the rep before you do. This will not only prevent your perspectives from influencing the team's feedback but will also help reinforce critical peer coaching behaviors.

After running this exercise hundreds of times with my clients, I can tell you that one of the biggest surprises you'll notice is how consistently positive, constructive, and encouraging the peer feedback is. Not only does it inspire the reps to continue to refine their tactics, but it also reduces the amount of emotional capital, ego, and fear the reps bring to the exercise. It won't take long for reps to quickly volunteer to have their calls reviewed because of how valuable and motivating the experience is!

Ninja Circle

This simple approach harkens back to the 1980s and early 1990s, when movies featuring ninjas were most popular. Many of these movies featured a climactic scene where the hero was ultimately surrounded by an army of shadowy ninjas who proceeded to politely attack one at a time and were summarily dispatched in the same order. In a group setting, simply have one rep play the hero and have their peers "attack" them with relevant random questions and objections to which they must immediately respond.

Deputize Your Team

In one particular year, I found myself in a bit of a leadership predicament. I was leading seven teams at the time, each with its own manager. The problem was that I started the year one manager short. So while we recruited that final leader, I had to directly manage all the reps on that team in addition to leading the larger region. To top it all off, I was based in Toronto, and all of the reps in the manager-less team were in New York.

I traveled to the New York office at least once a month to spend time with them, but the responsibility and pressure of doing two jobs was tough, and I didn't feel I was doing either as well as I could. To help ease the burden, I decided to share some of my leadership responsibilities with the team. Little did I realize that what I ended up doing out of necessity turned out to be a powerful approach with many benefits when it came to fostering a culture of mutual accountability.

To begin with, I identified leadership responsibilities that other team members could take on. For example, one of the reps could be responsible for sourcing all the data needed to craft the weekly sales forecast on time. Another could compile all the relevant marketing updates the team needed to be aware of. And another could provide educational updates to the team about current events and industry news that were relevant to our customers.

I also involved the team in the process, asking them what additional roles and responsibilities they felt would be helpful that they could take on. They suggested having someone responsible for deciding how to use our monthly spiff and promotions budget to incentivize the team and officiate the process. Another would coordinate group social outings, and another would plan customer events in the region. Responsibilities were rotated among team members each month, giving them a chance to take on different roles over time.

Besides preserving more of my bandwidth and ensuring the team ran smoothly when I wasn't present in the office, the approach is powerful for a number of important reasons:

1   **IT DRIVES MUTUAL ACCOUNTABILITY:** It's one thing for your reps to feel accountable to you. It's another for them to feel accountable to each other. The desire not to let their peers down not only creates a strong sense of trust between team members but also promotes a high degree of compliance to the asks they make of each other as part of their roles.

2   **IT PROMOTES OWNERSHIP AND COMPLIANCE:** When people get to make their own suggestions or recommendations versus being told what to do, they feel a greater sense of ownership of the ideas. That makes it much more likely they'll follow through on them. By incorporating the team's role suggestions into the approach, you get them to be more committed to the process. We'll dive deeper into this powerful concept as we explore coaching tactics in chapter 5.

3   **IT BUILDS IMPORTANT DELEGATION SKILLS:** Many leaders struggle to let go of responsibility and delegate tasks effectively. Deputizing helps you build that competency. Effective delegation isn't about passing off work or shirking responsibility; it's about recognizing the strengths and talents of your team members, giving them opportunities to flex those muscles, and using their expertise to achieve the best outcome.

4   **IT HELPS GROOM FUTURE LEADERS:** Part of your role as a leader is to inspire and prepare others to take up the mantle. By deputizing your team and sharing your leadership responsibilities, you provide much-needed practice and visibility into what it takes to be successful in the role. As an added benefit, it also gives your team a deeper appreciation for how challenging your role can be at times,

increasing their degree of empathy for all the leadership skills we're exploring in this book.

5 **IT HELPS YOU LEARN MORE ABOUT YOUR TEAM:** Beyond seeing how your reps operate as micro-leaders, providing them with the autonomy to make certain decisions can give you helpful insights into your team's culture. For example, in consultation with the team, the rep responsible for spiff and promotions on my New York team devised a contest for generating the most pipeline that month. The surprising reward for the winner? An afternoon off, out of the office, to run key errands and attend personal appointments. I didn't get it. "An afternoon off?" I questioned. "That seems like a strange reward. You're all adults, and I trust you to manage your work schedules and stay on top of your activities. As long as you do that, I don't mind if you leave the office in the afternoon for an important errand or appointment." What I didn't appreciate at the time was the tight-knit culture within the New York team that fueled that choice of reward. The spiff leader explained, "The thing is, we have a bit of a code here. We're all in the office every day, hustling, making calls, working with customers, and support-ing each other. While one of us *could* take an afternoon off to do personal things, it would feel like we're breaking that code and the commitment we've made to the team. By having the prize be an afternoon off, it gives us permission to break the code." It was a powerful reminder that, as leaders, we can't always see the forces driving our team. But taking the time to understand and tap into them is often worth the investment.

If you're interested in trying this deputizing strategy with your team, start by drawing a simple three-column chart like the one to follow. Then list some role titles and key leadership responsibilities associated with each of them. Share your intentions with your team and solicit some of their suggestions for the same. From there you can either assign roles to specific team members or ask for volunteers to assume them. Remember, the roles and responsibilities can be rotated among team members based on their strengths and interests so that each member has a chance to contribute and cultivate these important skills.

Role Title	Key Responsibilities	Team Member

When and How to Dial It Up

As we round out our conversation on accountability, it's important to note that the scope and level of intensity of this critical skill can and should vary depending on the needs of your operation. For example, when it comes to scope, we've seen that accountability is certainly something that can be driven at the individual level, such as when a rep needs to boost their production of outbound prospecting activities or proficiency in delivering their corporate pitch. But it can also exist at the team level, like when you're driving attainment toward a group pipeline or revenue quota, inspiring collective hustle on a call blitz, or deputizing your direct reports with shared leadership responsibilities.

Expanding the sphere of accountability even further, you can bring stakeholders outside your team and across your organization into the mix. For example, we saw in chapter 1, when we explored the concept of trust and the value of quality relationships, that as our quota period draws to a close, our reliance on our internal support network within our company grows. That means that not only do we rely on our colleagues in legal, revenue operations, professional services, and engineering to get deals done, but if the organization as a whole has a focus on hitting revenue targets (which most do), the best sales leaders also play a key role in mobilizing their corporate partners toward that collective goal with shared accountability.

Intensity is the second dimension that can be moderated when it comes to accountability. In general, the approaches we covered in the section about letting data do the hard work would be considered light to medium, whereas promoting ongoing practice would be medium to heavy due to the live presence required. But even within these frameworks, intensity can be easily moderated to suit the need. For example, if you find that too many of your team's opportunities are extending beyond your typical sales cycle length, you might choose to include an "opportunity age" metric on a CRM dashboard to provide visibility into deals that might be going stale. However, if you find that aging pipeline is a chronic and high-impact issue for your team, consider amping up the level of accountability. For instance, shift from a light to medium intensity by sending proactive notifications to specific reps when the average age of their pipeline or a given opportunity crosses a predetermined age threshold. If you find that's still not enough, consider invoking heavier doses of accountability by devoting time in your regular team meetings to discussing this metric and the tactics each member of your team is using to get things back on track.

The intensity/scope accountability matrix shown here provides some examples of how these two dimensions can be moderated to drive accountability for sales pipeline generation.

In the matrix, the numbers represent the following activities:

1　Set a pipeline generation goal for a single rep in a one-on-one coaching conversation.

2　Display individuals' pipeline generation numbers on the team dashboard.

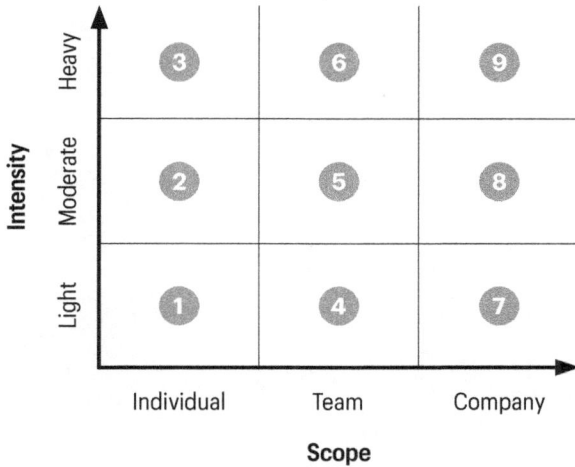

3   Set a formal pipeline target to maintain employment as part of an individual's performance improvement plan.

4   Set a monthly pipeline generation goal for the team.

5   Organize a weekly, team-wide prospecting call blitz.

6   Organize a weekly, team-wide prospecting call blitz with targets by product and customer profile.

7   Establish an ongoing, company-wide customer referral bonus program.

8   Set company-wide pipeline generation goals by group or role (e.g., sales, marketing, account management).

9   Hold a month-long, cross-departmental pipeline generation contest, with daily email updates.

Of course, if meaningful change is what you're after, applying focus on a specific metric, skill, or behavior in a one-on-one setting can be one of the most effective ways to get there. That's what we'll be discussing in the next chapter.

5

SKILL 4

Coaching
Your Team

The Case for Sales Coaching

The sales enablement universe is riddled with data evangelizing the virtues of sales coaching. For example:

- Sales coaching and mentoring are cited as the most important roles that frontline managers play, according to 74 percent of leading companies.

- In a 2021 survey, 96 percent of respondents either agreed or strongly agreed that effective sales coaching positively impacted their salespeople's performance.

- Of top-performing sales reps, 60 percent have weekly one-on-one coaching sessions with their managers, versus 34 percent of low performers.

- Sales reps with at least two hours of coaching per week have win rates 30 percent higher than reps who receive thirty minutes or less of sales coaching per week.

- Companies with tailored sales coaching programs aligned to their enablement strategy achieve 32 percent higher win rates.

- Companies that provide quality coaching can achieve 17 percent greater annual revenue growth.

What's more, in a role notorious for high turnover, sales coaching is a powerful retention lever. According to a survey conducted by *Harvard Business Review*, the annual turnover rate of salespeople in the United States is 27 percent, double the rate of all labor groups. And Salesforce's 2022 *State of Sales* report stated that nearly one in four reps was either looking or planning to look for a new job within twelve months, with nearly half being open to leaving. Of course, there are many factors that play into that statistic, such as the burnout created by constant quota pressure, challenging work/life balance, and poor company culture. But in a world where 96 percent of employees say it's important or very important for them to continuously develop their work-related skills, it should come as no surprise that upwards of 60 percent of employees say they're more likely to leave their job if their manager is a poor coach.

With almost no other productivity investment representing the same rate of return as good sales coaching, you'd think sales leaders would be scrambling to master, prioritize, and execute this critical behavior. But you would be wrong.

Coaching Conundrum

A study by the Sales Management Association found that a staggering 77 percent of companies do not provide enough coaching to their salespeople. And of the coaching that is provided, more than half of all companies categorize it as slightly to completely ineffective. It's not surprising, then, that according to another study, 82 percent of sales leaders believe they're providing their reps with coaching, but only 48 percent of salespeople report feeling like they are getting coached. What's even worse is that when sales managers are perceived as being poor coaches, their reps may end up losing their appetite for the experience. Research from Bain & Company showed that less than half of reps would be willing to pay at least one dollar for an hour of their manager's coaching time.

This coaching conundrum is caused by multiple issues.

Issue 1: We Don't Prioritize It

On the sales floor, one of the biggest reasons salespeople suffer from low close rates and poor forecast accuracy is that they fail to create a sense of urgency in the minds of their customers. And when it comes to creating—or at least uncovering—urgency, one of the most critical but subtle mistakes salespeople make is focusing too heavily on business cases for their solution and not nearly enough on their customer's emotional motivators for wanting to solve the problem. In other words, they confuse two critical but very different concepts: importance and priority.

Importance speaks to the magnitude of the problem a customer is looking to solve. Priority is the customer's sense of urgency to solve it. For example, you might say your health is very important to you. Yet, if I were to follow you around for a week and record what you ate, how you spent your time, and noted your exercise regimen, my observations might tell a different story about the priority you place on your health. In the same way, sales leaders might agree that coaching their reps is extremely important. But in the face of massive quota pressures, operational distractions, and endless internal meetings, this valuable activity gets deprioritized.

Maura Thomas is an award-winning speaker on individual and corporate productivity, attention management, and work/life balance.

She states that leaders often give this lament:

> I believe in the power of mentoring and coaching my team members. The most important thing I can do as a leader is support them and encourage their growth. [Then] I spend a big chunk of my time on email and putting out fires. I started the year with a coaching plan for my team, but it's fallen by the wayside amid everything else that is going on. My one-on-ones with team members don't happen as often as I would like, and the content is too much "trees" and not enough "forest."

Like spending quality time with your family, getting regular exercise, or taking a vacation to recharge your emotional batteries, if you believe coaching is important, it must be given priority. That means it needs to be not only inscribed but defended in your schedule.

Issue 2: We Lack Diagnostic and Accountability Frameworks

Suppose you felt you could spend a little more time on improving your level of physical fitness. After all, you know how important that investment is. So you finally decide to prioritize getting that gym membership you've been putting off and make an effort to go a few times a week. You start off strong with a high degree of resolve. Of course, you're not quite sure what to do or which exercises are best suited to your needs and goals. You bounce between the cardio machines, free weights, and floor exercises. You try keeping up the pace, but after a month or two you're struggling to find traction. You come to the gym without a plan, not knowing how to get the results you're after. A short time later you find yourself attending less frequently for shorter periods of time. At this point, you feel like you're just going through the motions. Finally, you find yourself in the same position as 67 percent of Americans, paying for a gym membership you no longer use to the collective tune of $397 million per year. For most sales leaders and their teams, this is precisely how their coaching journey ends.

The role of the sales leader is similar to that of a personal trainer. Your job is not to lift the weights for your team members, but rather to guide them on the journey that gets them the results they're after and highlight the progress they're making along the way. In order to do that, you need a system to consistently diagnose the needs of the individual, the ability to craft a plan that engages them in the right behaviors, and a mechanism to hold them accountable. Without this framework in place, neither you nor your team will stick to the coaching regimen in the long term.

Issue 3: We Tell Instead of Lead

One of the reasons for the gap in perception between reps and leaders when it comes to whether or not coaching is happening is the difference between what each group considers coaching to be. Some leaders think of coaching as a mentoring practice where the rep's performance is monitored and analyzed and areas for behavioral improvement are identified through collaborative discussion. Others might consider it to be a directive exercise where reps are evaluated and provided with specific instructions to drive more consistent and sustained sales performance. As it turns out, your perspective here depends on where you sit within the organization.

A large-scale study of 2,000 global leaders found both encouraging and concerning trends when it came to coaching. On the positive side, three-quarters of the leaders surveyed preferred to manage through collaborative, discovery-based mentoring interactions with their team members. But when the researchers examined the data by job title, they found that more senior leaders such as C-level executives and vice presidents had a stronger bias toward these positive coaching behaviors. By contrast, frontline leaders such as managers and supervisors were more likely to engage in directive leadership—favoring providing instructions and advice over collaboration. While this type of autocratic leadership can be efficient and produce results, more often it produces unexpected negative consequences.

As we discussed in chapter 1, predictability is one of the key traits of great leaders. But it can also be a key trait of those who fail to motivate and inspire their team. Leaders who are predictably directive often succeed in conditioning their teams to either wait for their orders or come to them for every single decision. This results in a decline in their initiative and overall engagement and longer decision cycles, sitting at odds with everyone's objectives. By contrast, a predictably collaborative coaching style can both save leaders time and boost engagement.

Over the years, when a team member came to me with a problem and asked, "What do you think we should do?" my favorite and highly predictable response was, "I don't know. What do *you* think we should do?" That's why one of my most memorable leadership moments was the first time a rep came to me for advice and opened with, "David, I have a problem that I'd love your advice on. Now, I know you're going to ask me what *I* think we should do, so let me explain the problem and how I'm thinking of solving it." If your goal is to become the type of leader your team would fight to work with again by helping them grow and unlocking their discretionary effort, predictably biasing toward the collaborative mode of coaching is the approach you're after.

Counterpoint: When Is Directive Coaching OK?

When I was interviewing for a vice president of commercial sales role, Tony Rodoni, who at the time was the executive vice president of our division, asked me a question about the balance of directive versus collaborative coaching. He said, "David, I know as leaders we strive to coach our reps and lead them to the answers they need. But under what circumstances do you think it might be OK to just tell them what to do?" Indeed, there are periodic instances when directive leadership makes sense. For example:

1 **SECURITY, REGULATORY, OR COMPLIANCE-BASED SCENARIOS:** When there are strict rules and guidelines the team needs to follow, being more directive ensures the team both follows those rules and appreciates their importance. These might include things like the protocols for executing and processing sales agreements, making changes to legal terms and other official documents, or human resources procedures related to recruiting or termination conduct.

2 **SALES PROCESS AND METHODOLOGY:** Most sales organizations have a defined sales process and methodology that the team must follow. In some instances, members might require guidance and direction on how to execute the process effectively. In others, leaders may be instructing team members on precisely how to implement these frameworks in an online platform. In these instances, a directive leadership style can help to ensure the team is following the right steps and using the appropriate techniques to drive revenue.

3 **NEW OR INEXPERIENCED TEAM MEMBERS:** When new or inexperienced team members join the team, they may need more guidance and direction to understand how to do their job effectively. Many procedures, directives, and instructions are often provided in the form of onboarding and enablement resources. But in many cases, it's reasonable for leaders to give these reps more hands-on direction in their early days to show them, as we've already discussed, what "good" looks like. As the team member gains more experience and confidence, the leader can shift to a more collaborative coaching style.

4   **URGENT, TIME-SENSITIVE, AND CRITICAL SITUATIONS:** When urgent and critical situations arise, such as a negotiation roadblock on a large deal hours before the end of a quarter or a major customer threatening to cancel their contract, there may not be time for the team to brainstorm and come up with a solution. In these situations, it's reasonable for leaders to be more directive by providing clear and immediate suggestions or solutions.

Warning: Don't Play Super Rep!

Beware! Providing direction and assuming control are two different things. Donning your cape, pushing your way into your team's deals, and taking on the role of the "Super Rep" when things aren't going according to plan may seem necessary on the surface, but engaging in this behavior repeatedly and in the wrong way can have negative consequences, including these:

1   **STUNTED LEARNING:** If you constantly rescue your sales reps, not only will you condition them to be rescued, but they'll also struggle to learn essential skills for overcoming obstacles. Give them room to navigate tough situations with your guidance, not by assuming total control.

2   **STRAINED TRUST:** Taking over deals can make your team members believe you don't trust their skills and experience. This creates unnecessary tension and leads to decreased team morale and loyalty, ultimately limiting your growth and development as a leader.

3   **LIMITING YOUR IMPACT:** As a sales leader, you should spend your time on activities that help you scale your impact across the team. When you become too focused and involved in individual deals, you reduce your focus on process improvement and creating the strong infrastructure needed to set your team up for long-term success.

Urgent interventions should be used sparingly and in a way that doesn't undermine the relationship between the rep, yourself, and the customer.

Diagnosing Issues: Top-Down Sales Coaching

Your ability to diagnose issues in your team's funnel and how they execute in the field is critical. This doesn't mean you, as a sales leader, need to be a better salesperson than everyone on your team or possess an instinctive ability to identify their problems. After all, the "best sales leader you ever had" exercise we explored in chapter 1 didn't feature "masterful selling prowess" as a key qualification for that title. However, it does mean that leaders need to have a consistent system to cut through the noise, figure out what's going on, uncover the root causes, and prescribe a course of treatment.

Like a doctor diagnosing a patient, sales leaders have a variety of tools, tests, and tricks they can use to get the insights they're looking for. And as with a doctor, these tools are not meant to be used in isolation. The ability to use data, listen, understand key trends and patterns, and ask the right questions is critical for their success. In the sections that follow, we'll be discussing in detail the two macro ways to go about diagnosing your team's issues: top-down and bottom-up. We'll start with a simple formula for top-down sales coaching.

The Leading Indicators Coaching Formula

As a former engineer and research scientist, I have a simple and effective framework I love for sales coaching. Like a chemical reaction, it involves following the process of turning a sales activity into a qualified opportunity, all the way through to closed business, and ultimately to the growth of that account's revenue through renewal, cross-sell, and upsell activities. In fact, this is precisely how the sales process in many

CRM systems is configured. I call this the Leading Indicators Coaching Formula, and the equation for this reaction with the respective coefficients looks like this:

$$\text{Activity} \xrightarrow{\text{A}} \text{Pipeline} \xrightarrow{\text{B}} \text{Revenue} \xrightarrow{\text{C}} \text{Growth}$$

While the process itself reads from left to right, the coaching narrative reads from right to left. In other words:

Our ultimate goal is to have loyal customers with a high lifetime value because they continue to renew and grow their revenue footprint with us . . .

. . . but we have no expectation of account growth unless we close that initial round of revenue with the right customers, stay engaged with them, and deliver the value we initially promised (C) . . .

. . . and we have no expectation of revenue unless we first build enough qualified sales pipeline and progress those customers through the buying process efficiently (B) . . .

. . . and we have no expectation of a healthy sales pipeline unless we generate enough sales activities like prospecting calls, emails, customer meetings, and all the related follow-up actions (A).

Before we go further, it's important to note three things. First, in order for this top-down diagnostic framework to work, all of the categories should be things you can measure and report on, ideally from your CRM system. If you can't, it will be very difficult to accurately coach the right behaviors and hold your team accountable for them. Second, while the categories listed above will work for most sales environments, they can be changed based on the nature of your operation and role. For example, if you manage a team of sales or solution engineers, your formula might look like this:

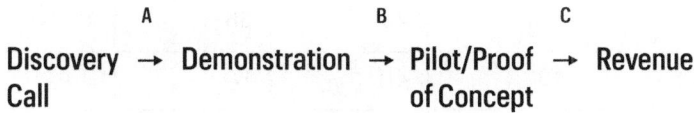

A   B   C

Discovery → Demonstration → Pilot/Proof → Revenue
Call   of Concept

If you manage a team of business development reps, your formula might look like this:

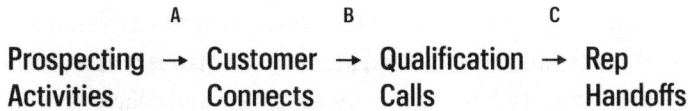

A   B   C

Prospecting → Customer → Qualification → Rep
Activities   Connects   Calls   Handoffs

And finally, while you might be tempted to make the framework more granular, it's best to start with a simple four-step process. This will help you identify the large-scale issues. From there, you can dive deeper.

Using the framework below, take a moment now to write down what this diagnostic Leading Indicators Coaching Formula would look like for your team or operation.

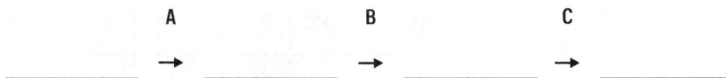

A   B   C

_____ → _____ → _____ → _____

Identifying Problem Areas

After you've crafted the formula that works for your business, the next step is to select the desired time horizon and source the data you need from each category. For example, consider the data for the four reps shown below from the first month of the year.

Rep	Activity (Calls)	Pipeline ($K)	Revenue ($K)	Growth ($K)
Les	425	431	36	10
Rona	400	411	17	9
Shane	412	109	9	2
Elise	53	3	0	0

By examining the values and the conversion rates from one stage of the process to another, you can identify at a glance where the bottlenecks might be and where further investigation and coaching attention are needed. In this scenario, we identified that each rep has an issue at a different point in the revenue funnel, as illustrated by the chart below.

Rep	Activity (Calls)		Pipeline ($K)		Revenue ($K)		Growth ($K)	
Les	425	✓	431	✓	36	✓	10	✗
Rona	400	✓	411	✓	17	✗	9	✗
Shane	412	✓	109	✗	9	✗	2	✗
Elise	53	✗	3	✗	0	✗	0	✗

Depending on how your sales organization is structured, it might also be helpful to look at this framework at a higher level, such as by team, region, or the company overall.

Region	Activity (Calls)	Pipeline ($K)	Revenue ($K)	Growth ($K)
West	914	3,254	304	116
Central	1,195	3,985	318	95
East	1,326	4,255	391	147

Region	Activity (Calls)		Pipeline ($K)		Revenue ($K)		Growth ($K)	
West	914	✓	3,254	✗	304	✗	116	✗
Central	1,195	✓	3,985	✓	318	✗	95	✗
East	1,326	✓	4,255	✓	391	✓	147	✓

Before moving to the analysis stage, it's important to note the time-dependent nature of this data. In other words, even though we're using a simple four-step revenue lifecycle to illustrate this process, the timeframe during which this data is captured may be different from the time it takes for sales activities to move through the lifecycle for your business.

For example, suppose you had a tomato garden. Measuring how many tomato seeds you planted in your garden this month relative to how many actual tomatoes you harvested from fully mature plants during the same month may not make sense. After all, the tomatoes you picked today came from seeds that were planted and cultivated in prior months. In the same way, the revenue your team secures this month could have started life as a cold outreach activity many months ago (depending on the length of your sales cycle).

This means you have a few choices when it comes to analyzing and interpreting the data:

1   **ORGANIZE THE FRAMEWORK INTO COHORTS:** Start by looking at the metric on the left-hand side of the formula and follow it through your funnel, focused on that cohort. For example, if your average sales cycle is ninety days, look at the activities generated ninety days ago and follow the leads associated with those specific activities through to revenue. You can then analyze the data within the same cohort and even compare conversion rates for specific steps between cohorts to examine how the bottlenecks change. Many systems have built-in reports that do this automatically for you.

2   **ZOOM IN AND EVALUATE PORTIONS OF THE FRAMEWORK:** Rather than looking at the entire cycle, look at a smaller portion of it where the time dependencies are less important. For example, the time between when a cold call or email to a prospect occurs and when they are converted to a qualified lead in your pipeline may be small relative to the overall cycle. Therefore, looking at the conversion from one step to another within the same reporting period is still meaningful even if the data isn't organized by cohort. Alternatively, you might compare that conversion rate across two different reporting periods (e.g., from Q1 to Q2) to see how the statistic is trending.

3   **ZOOM OUT AND LOOK AT THE BIGGER PICTURE:** Speaking as a former research scientist who specialized in creating mathematical computer models, there is no doubt that the first two options provide more satisfying doses of scientific rigor. But practically speaking, point-in-time snapshots of the entire framework can still provide more than enough direction to fuel your coaching conversations. This is especially true if your analysis time horizon is long

enough to capture cohorts across multiple stages. For example, if the average cycle represented by your top-down model is sixty days long, examining the data for a period such as a fiscal quarter, half year, or year is more than adequate. So when in doubt, don't worry about getting too fancy with your approach. Start simple, run the numbers across the time horizon you feel makes the most sense, identify the potential bottleneck, and use those insights to dive deeper with your reps to isolate and validate the rate-limiting behaviors.

Once you've identified the areas in which the bottlenecks lie, you can begin to diagnose what might be causing them. This involves identifying the typical operational and execution issues most associated with the transition from one stage to the next.

Rep	Activity (Calls)		Pipeline ($K)		Revenue ($K)		Growth ($K)		Investigation Point
Les	425	✓	431	✓	36	✓	10	✗	C
Rona	400	✓	411	✓	17	✗	9	✗	B
Shane	412	✓	109	✗	9	✗	2	✗	A
Elise	53	✗	3	✗	0	✗	0	✗	0

Problems Retaining and Growing Revenue

Suppose you see lots of activity, pipeline, and revenue, but very few of your customers are renewing their agreements or growing their revenue footprint with you. You would start to investigate what's happening in the "C" portion of the Leading Indicators Coaching Formula process. That means once the customer signs, deploys, and uses your product or service, you might explore diagnostic questions like these:

- Did the rep oversell the customer or misrepresent the capabilities of our solution?

- Did we not support the customer correctly after the sale?

- Did we not identify the right champion? Did that person leave?

- Did our solution not deliver on the value promise made during the sales cycle?

In my last role as VP of sales, I used the forensic approach outlined in the previous section when investigating the topic of customer churn and net revenue retention, a prevalent issue for us. Specifically, the renewal conversion rate across my team members was average, with the exception of one particular rep, whose success in this area stood out. I decided to bring this surprising trend to the rep in a coaching conversation and asked what he felt he was doing differently than the rest of the team to achieve such a positive result. He told me that beyond enabling his customer-side champions to make the case for our solution internally, he went a step further. He found specific champions who could tether the success of their career to the successful implementation and ongoing management of our solution internally. By creating this deep, emotional linkage with the customer, he was able to significantly increase their retention, renewal, and growth, boosting this key metric for our business. We went on to share this tactic with the rest of our team as a powerful example of this diagnostic approach.

Problems Executing and Closing Opportunities

Suppose you see lots of activity and pipeline, but less revenue than you expect resulting from that pipeline. You would start looking at what's happening in the "B" portion of the process, examining how good your reps are at winning the business they've identified as legitimate opportunities. If the conversion rate is low (as it usually is when revenue output is suffering), you might explore diagnostic questions like these:

- Does the rep have challenges with the accuracy of their forecast? If so, why?

- Were the opportunities the rep identified real or a good fit to begin with?

- Are we experiencing competitive threats from other vendors?

- Are we losing more deals or simply more revenue through excessive discounting?

To help diagnose issues and coaching opportunities in this stage of the sales funnel, digging deeper into the data can be very helpful. For example, if you track loss or reason codes in your CRM when a rep closes out an opportunity prematurely (which you should be), aggregate and report on them to see if you can spot a trend. Are deals being lost due to the absence of a specific solution, integration capability, or feature set? Are we losing because our pricing model doesn't scale to the scope our customers require? Or are we having challenges winning business with customers of a particular size, either large or small?

Diving deeper, it's also helpful to examine the stage at which your reps' opportunities are falling out of the funnel. To do this, I often started my analysis by running the insightful "stage-to-dead" report I mentioned in chapter 4. That report looked at all the dead opportunities a rep or group had in a given time period and asked the question, "What stage were they at before they died?"

The coaching opportunities you identify will depend on where the majority of the rep's deals are falling off. For example:

Early-stage losses:

- Do we have an issue with the quality and consistency of leads coming through our marketing and business development channels?

- Is the rep struggling to craft a compelling narrative to move deals forward?

- Is the rep unable to set high-value next steps that progress the opportunity?

Middle-stage losses:

- Has the rep identified the right buyers and decision-makers within the customer's organization?

- Has the rep sufficiently demonstrated to the customer how our solution would solve their specific problem?

- Is the rep struggling to uncover the customer's source of urgency or craft a compelling business case for why they should move forward?

Late-stage losses:

- Did we miss an important competitive threat that would have caused a late-stage shift in direction?

- Are senior customer stakeholders—like executives, board members, and venture capitalists—who we failed to engage earlier in the process killing the deal during the final approval steps?

- Is this *really* a late-stage loss, or did the rep advance the deal prematurely, skipping steps and not sufficiently qualifying the opportunity in the earlier stages?

Problems Engaging and Qualifying Opportunities

Suppose you see your reps engaging in lots of activity, but those activities aren't producing enough pipeline. You would start to investigate what's happening in the initial, "A" portion of the process. Diagnosing the issue might lead you to ask questions like these:

- Is the rep biasing too strongly toward one type of prospecting activity (e.g., too much drive-by social media pitching and not enough cold calling)?

- Is the rep doing enough research before attempting to connect with the prospect? Are they seen as bothersome and too pushy and being ignored?

- What are they saying in their outreach? Is their messaging sharp and crisp? Are they trying to communicate too much information about our solutions as opposed to enticing the customer to engage in a conversation?

- Is the rep not calling into the right person or role within the customer organization? Or is their message not aligned with the person or role they're reaching out to?

- Are they asking for too much of a commitment from their customers early in the process?

- Are they calling on too many existing clients at the cost of prospecting into new ones?

NOTE: A great way to refine these tactics is to promote accountability for regular practice using the tactics we covered in chapter 4.

I've worked with many clients experiencing challenges in this stage of the process. For example, a rep at a software company told me that he was using video messages to entice prospects with his value proposition and drive them to a discovery call. Unfortunately, he wasn't having much success and was confused as to why. When I listened to his video messages, the reason became clear. Even though his recordings were relatively short (a good thing), his messaging and, more importantly, his call-to-action at the end were all wrong. He began his narrative with an overview of his solution instead of focusing on the problem his customer was likely experiencing. Then he ended the video by asking the prospect to schedule a forty-five-minute discovery call with him. Without deepening the customer's interest in solving their problem, the massive ask of time for a meeting of unknown value was clearly scaring his prospects away.

Problems Generating Enough Activity

And finally, what happens if you don't see enough activity? Well, let's just say that pipeline and revenue don't generate themselves! But the absence of foundational sales activity and hustle can point to a number of root causes, raising diagnostic questions like these:

- Does the rep not have enough accounts or prospects to call on?
- Have we crafted our territories and identified our ideal customer profile incorrectly?
- Does the rep lack an understanding of what a good-fit prospect looks like?
- Does the rep lack the confidence and conviction to reach out to customers due to insufficient training or practice?
- Is the rep not engaged in their role, checked out, or looking for a job elsewhere?

If you find yourself coaching a rep through this type of challenge, there might also be a deeper, more personal issue at play here—things that can't be easily seen on a dashboard or report. For example, they might be distracted because they're dealing with a personal issue such as a painful relationship breakup, a concerning medical diagnosis, a tragedy related to a close friend or relative, or other emotional trauma. That means to uncover and explore these issues, and more, you'll need to rely on the relationship and trust you've built with your team using the approaches we've covered in this book so far. With that foundation in place, it's possible to take a more bottom-up, discovery-based approach to coaching. Here we can learn what might be holding our reps back and help them improve by asking thoughtful questions in much the same way we do with our customers. That's what we'll be covering in the sections to come.

Putting It All Together

While the Leading Indicators Coaching Formula can be a powerful diagnostic tool, it also has three additional key benefits:

1 **RAMPING NEW HIRES EFFICIENTLY:** Coaching a new rep using this formula helps provide the initial structure and focus they require to succeed in your environment. That's because, in the early days, you're less concerned about the end result and more focused on helping new reps build the right foundational habits and behaviors. Focusing on the leading indicators of success and getting at-bats with customers is critical. As they achieve higher degrees of mastery in those activities, you can shift your enablement efforts further down the formula.

2 **SELF-DIAGNOSING ISSUES:** Because this approach is so simple and the data can be made widely available (as we discussed in chapter 4, where we let data do the hard work), reps can use it themselves to diagnose bottlenecks in their own sales motion. Armed with these insights, they can come to your coaching sessions prepared, ready to discuss their challenges and potential solutions to address them.

Not only can this save you time, but it can also help develop the rep's muscle memory for this important analytical skill.

3 **INFORMING ENABLEMENT AND INTERDEPARTMENTAL STRATEGIES:** When you aggregate the insights from this model across your team members, region, or company, it will provide you with valuable perspectives on where you should focus your enablement efforts and how to collaborate better with other departments. For example, on the one hand, you might find that many of your team members are struggling to uncover their customer's sense of urgency to solve their problem (which, as we learned earlier in this chapter, is different and more critical than its importance). In that case, some targeted sales training on the topic might be in order. On the other hand, perhaps your analysis points to an issue with the lead qualification and handoff process from your marketing team or how projects are transitioned to your implementation, service partner, or customer support teams once signed. This top-down diagnostic approach can help you refine your strategies for working with team members outside your department.

Before you move on, take a moment to complete a model of what the Leading Indicators Coaching Formula might look like for your team or operation. That means, in addition to the stages themselves, indicate what potential skill or training gaps might exist at each stage and the coaching questions you might explore with your reps to help diagnose the root causes behind the bottlenecks you're seeing.

A		B		C	
_____	→	_____	→	_____	→	_____

Step	Potential Skill/ Training Gap	Diagnostic Coaching Questions
0		
A		
B		
C		

For example, combining the concepts we've covered so far, our model might look something like this:

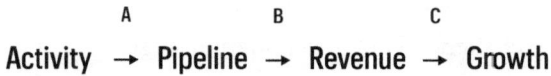

$$\text{Activity} \xrightarrow{A} \text{Pipeline} \xrightarrow{B} \text{Revenue} \xrightarrow{C} \text{Growth}$$

Step 0

POTENTIAL SKILL/TRAINING GAPS

- Motivation
- Engagement
- Time management

DIAGNOSTIC COACHING QUESTIONS

- Is the rep not engaged in their work?
- Is the rep too distracted by low-value tasks?
- Are there issues outside of work that are interfering?

Step A

POTENTIAL SKILL/TRAINING GAPS

- Prospecting
- Messaging, value definition
- Mindset/low conviction

DIAGNOSTIC COACHING QUESTIONS
- Is the rep reaching out at the right time?
- What is the rep saying on their calls or in their emails?
- Is the rep operating with high conviction?

Step B
POTENTIAL SKILL/TRAINING GAPS
- Discovery/qualification
- Negotiation
- Consistency of process

DIAGNOSTIC COACHING QUESTIONS
- Where are the deals falling out of the funnel?
- Was the pipeline real to begin with?
- Is the rep challenged in the negotiation stages?

Step C
POTENTIAL SKILL/TRAINING GAPS
- Managing expectations
- Transitioning from sales
- Identifying champion

DIAGNOSTIC COACHING QUESTIONS
- Did the rep oversell the customer?
- Did we not support the customer correctly post-sale?
- Did we not identify the right champion? Did they leave?

Diagnosing Issues: Bottom-Up Coaching Discovery

As we've already seen, coaching your team by diagnosing issues with their performance using a top-down approach can be very helpful, but it's not always sufficient. This is especially true when it comes to uncovering insights that can't be measured on a report or dashboard. That's where bottom-up discovery comes in. Here we coach reps and expose opportunities for growth by asking them probing questions, similar to how we engage in discovery conversations with our customers. The sections below outline some of the most powerful questions of this variety.

How Are You? (But Ask Twice)

Asking someone how they're doing is one of the best and easiest ways to start a coaching conversation. The problem is that we get asked how we are so often that we've become desensitized to the question. From the cashier in the supermarket checkout to telemarketers, everyday people use it as a casual greeting or formality. And, if you're like most of us when asked, you typically respond with "Good," or "I'm fine, thank you," even when you're not. After all, most of the people who ask us this question actually don't care about how we are. That's why as a sales coach you need to double down on it.

Canadian professional tennis player Bianca Andreescu rose to fame after defeating Serena Williams in the championship match of the 2019 US Open. But in late 2021, Andreescu announced she was stepping away from tennis after two challenging years of injuries and mental health issues during the COVID-19 pandemic. In a televised interview just prior to Andreescu's return in April 2022, CBC reporter Andrew Chang began the conversation with a simple, "Hey there, Bianca, how are you?" to which the star enthusiastically responded, "Very good! I'm training well, I'm healthy, and I'm looking forward to my first tournament back." An answer most viewers would be happy with. But knowing that Andreescu's journey was fraught with adversity, instead of continuing with his line of questioning, Chang paused, leaned in, and in a slow and concerned tone said, "Can I ask you about the road to getting back? Because you've had a lot of ups and downs. So maybe I'll ask you the very first question I asked you again.

How are you?" Seemingly taken aback by the genuine sense of caring and curiosity, Andreescu responded, "Yeah, it's definitely been a bunch of challenges, some struggles, and a lot of tears, but I'm good now."

When you're coaching your team from a genuine sense of caring, empathy, and understanding, you want to create a safe space for them to share their true feelings. As if you're saying, "I know people ask you how you're doing all the time, but knowing how you *really* are is important to me." So if you fear you're getting a canned "I'm good" response, don't be afraid to ask twice.

Jenny Brennan is a senior sales director who uses a powerful variation of this question with her team. In coaching conversations, she encourages her reps to open up by asking them to complete the sentence, "I'm good, but ..." By using this approach, she assumes (often correctly) that everyone has something in their lives, either personal or professional, that might be weighing on them. By inviting open dialogue and allowing her team to answer how they wish, she's able to better understand their perspectives and help them along their journey.

On a Scale of One to Ten...?

In *Sell the Way You Buy*, I talk about a powerful sales discovery framework in which you ask your customer to rate something on a scale of one to ten; for example, the amount of pain their situation is causing, their degree of happiness with their current vendor, or their sense of urgency to solve the problem in question. The reason these types of questions are so engaging is that, as research has found, people are psychologically predisposed to answering questions that require them to state their own views and opinions on things. This question framework plays right into that.

For example, in your coaching conversations, you might ask a rep, "On a scale of one to ten ..."

- "... how happy are you in your role?"

- "... how confident are you handling price objections?"

- "... how comfortable are you positioning the value of our new products?"

- "... how easy would you say the discount approval process is at our company?"

- "... how effective do you think your outbound cold-calling techniques are?"

And it doesn't matter what their answer is. The purpose of this approach is to start a conversation and get a sense of what the rep's perspective is on a given topic.

HELPFUL FOLLOW-UP TACTIC: Depending on the question you ask, the rep might be tempted to give a "safe" answer. For example, suppose you asked, "On a scale of one to ten, how prepared do you feel to move up a segment and start selling to larger customers?" Your rep might say "seven," making the response harder to interpret. If that happens, challenge them with this follow-up: "If it wasn't a seven, would it be a six or an eight?" Asking the rep to choose between a value one higher and lower will give you a better sense of which direction that trend is heading in.

What's Holding You Back?

As a sales leader, you share with your team members the goal of creating an environment free of barriers. One where everyone feels they're in a position to do their best work. But that doesn't mean everyone is. There are bound to be things your team feels are holding them back in general or in certain situations. And creating mutual awareness of what those things are will put you in a better position to coach and advocate for them, clearing the way for greater levels of engagement and productivity.

CORE VERSION: "What do you feel is holding you back from [insert thing]?"

That thing could be goals like these:

- Doing your best work
- Generating more sales pipeline
- Negotiating deals with fewer discounts
- Producing a more accurate sales forecast
- Being more prescriptive with your customers

In some ways, this question is similar to the exercise we explored in chapter 3, the One-Sentence Advocacy Builder; however, a couple of small modifiers can make this approach even more effective.

FOCUS MODIFIER: "What's the main thing you feel is holding you back from [insert thing]?"

Asking the question in this way assumes that many things could come to mind when you ask the rep what's holding them back. This phrasing forces the rep to pause, focus, and think about the single most important thing.

SITUATION MODIFIER: "What do you feel is holding you back from [insert thing] here?"

The thing holding them back (whether or not it's the main thing) could be situationally dependent. For example, the thing holding the rep back from giving away fewer discounts might depend on the type of customer they're selling to, the product they're selling, or the point during the month or quarter when the negotiation is happening. By adding a situational modifier to the question, you focus the coaching conversation on a highly specific set of circumstances. This can make the advice easier to act on.

You can also combine both modifiers for added impact.

COMBINATION MODIFIER: "What's the main thing you feel is holding you back from [insert thing] here?"

What Skill Can We Work On Together?

One of the key benefits of the coaching formula we discussed earlier is that its simplicity allows reps to self-diagnose issues in their sales funnel just by following the revenue journey. A natural extension of this process is having the rep consider what skills they might need to work on in order to bust through those roadblocks. In fact, asking the rep a question like "What skill can we help you develop together?" has three big benefits:

1 **SELF-AWARENESS:** It helps your reps develop a point of view on their own strengths and areas for improvement. This builds critical emotional intelligence skills and muscle memory for future self-reflection.

2 **COMMITMENT:** As we'll see in the next section, questions can be very powerful when it comes to driving commitment. When people come up with suggestions on their own, they are more likely to take ownership of them. In the same way, when a rep identifies a skill they'd like to work on and improve, the intrinsic feedback loop strengthens their commitment to the effort and outcome.

3 **ALIGNMENT:** It helps you determine how accurately your rep's assessment of their own needs aligns with where you see their opportunities for development. If you feel their perspective is misguided or they suggest focusing on a lower-value skill, you always have the ability to challenge, coach, and reframe their perspective using the approach we discussed earlier.

What Would You Do if Your Quota Was Doubled?

Promoting your team's focus is one of your most important jobs as a sales leader. With a weekly regimen of calls, meetings, demos, proposals, and prospecting activities, your reps can be easily caught up in activities that don't serve their goals. To help improve that focus, many leaders like to periodically ask their team members to consider what activities they should start, stop, and continue doing. But to avoid safe and simple choices and encourage your reps to step outside their comfort zone, consider raising the stakes by asking what they would do if the quota expectations placed on them were instantly doubled. Of course, you won't actually be doubling their quotas, but the stark contrast will catalyze conversations on more meaningful change.

Coaching for Commitment

As we conclude the conversation about top-down and bottom-up sales coaching, it's important to recognize that regardless of how you invoke these models, questions play an integral role in the interaction you have with your reps. In some cases, questions are used to validate and explore the trends the data is pointing you to. For example, if your analysis indicates your rep is getting stuck at the part of the sales cycle where the business case is being created, you might ask them questions like, "Would you agree this is where you're struggling?" "Why do you think this is happening?" or "Is there a particular part of the case your customers are getting hung up on?"

In other cases, questions are used to illuminate areas of opportunity and growth you can't see on a report: areas like mental health, career goals, the hidden forces holding them back, and the support they might need from you in order to move forward. But another reason questions are so powerful is their unique ability to drive alignment and commitment.

In 1997, the *New York Times* published an article titled "In War against No-Shows, Restaurants Get Tougher." It featured a Chicago restaurant that was facing a financial loss of $900,000 per year because a high number of customers weren't showing up for their reservations. The restaurant had initially attempted to fix the problem by politely requesting that patrons let them know if their plans changed. That approach didn't work, and the restaurant continued to experience a high no-show rate of 30 percent.

The breakthrough came when the restaurant staff decided to reframe their approach. They transformed their request into a question. "Please call us if you change your plans" became, "Will you call us if you change your plans?" This simple shift in wording had a profound impact. The no-show rates plummeted to just 10 percent.

This intriguing example underscores the power of using questions to influence behavior. By their very nature, questions need to be answered. And when they are, they prompt the responder to acknowledge the commitment they made, making them more likely to follow through. This phenomenon stems from people's intrinsic desire to reduce their cognitive dissonance: the inner conflict they have when it comes to aligning their attitudes, beliefs, and behaviors. In short, people are more committed to their ideas than yours. The same is true for sales coaching.

Helping Reps Own Their Goals

Suppose through your coaching conversations you and your sales rep identified a pipeline deficiency. To get back on track, the rep needs to increase the number of prospecting calls they make every week. They currently make about thirty calls, but you know that number should be closer to sixty. You can always just tell the rep they need to make sixty calls, and many leaders indeed take that prescriptive approach. But instead, you might decide to put the question back to the rep to increase their level of commitment to the action they need to take.

For example, you might say, "Eve, it sounds like you agree making thirty prospecting calls a week won't be enough to hit your revenue targets. Based on the conversion rate you're seeing from those calls, how many do you feel you should be making?" If Eve responds with something close to a reasonable number (e.g., fifty-five to sixty-five in this case), great! You would reply, "I think that number makes sense. Let's write it down in our coaching notes and revisit it at our one-on-one next week to make sure you're on track."

Even if the approach the rep suggests is slightly off pace from where you'd like it to be, it can still be better to let them set the bar. For example, suppose in the last scenario the rep suggested fifty-five prospecting calls. You pushing that number up to sixty may make the goal 8 percent better, but you'll end up reducing the rep's commitment to achieving that goal by 50 percent because they didn't come up with it themselves.

Of course, commitment is great when the things people are committing to make sense to us. But what happens if their insights or ideas are bad? For example, suppose you just finished an introductory call with a customer. At the end of the call, you asked them what they thought a good next step would be, and they responded, "Send me an email with some information and I'll let you know." Would you be happy with that answer? Do you feel like lobbing some PDFs over the wall and hoping the customer finds it in their heart to get back to you is the best way to move the deal forward? Of course not! The same thing can happen in your coaching conversations.

In the prospecting call scenario we just discussed, suppose the rep came back with a target of forty or even eighty calls. Both are problematic. The lower number won't have the desired impact, and the higher number may not be reasonably achievable at this stage. Here's where you can use what I call the "Kindergarten Classroom Rules" approach to reframe the rep's response.

You may not be able to remember what school was like at the age of five, but you can likely appreciate the tough task those who teach our youngest students have when it comes to managing classroom behavior. To keep the class in line, rather than bombard children with a formal list of rules, clever kindergarten teachers take a different approach. They sit their students down around the magic carpet, grab a colorful marker, walk up to a big white flipchart, and with a smile on their face, kick off a conversation that might sound something like this:

TEACHER: Now friends, just like at home, do you think it's important for us to have rules in our classroom to make sure everyone is safe and happy?

CLASSROOM [gleefully]: Yaaaaaaaa!

TEACHER: OK then! How about this? Since this is your classroom, why don't you make the rules and I'll write them down?

Here the teacher is taking precisely the same approach to coaching as a sales leader. By asking the class for input and moving forward with their suggestions, they're increasing the students' commitment to following the rules. After all, they're the class's rules, not the teacher's.

TEACHER: So friends, who has a suggestion for a rule we should have in our classroom?

KID #1 [raises hand]: We should share all the toys in the classroom with our friends!

TEACHER: I think that's a great rule. I'll write that down. Can anyone else think of another rule?

KID #2 [raises hand and laughs]: We should hit our friends if they don't share our toys with us!

The class laughs.

TEACHER: Oh, I'm not sure if hitting our friends is a good idea. What do you think everyone? Do we hit each other at our school?

CLASS [in unison]: Noooooooo!

TEACHER: OK then, I won't write that one down. What other rules can you come up with?

When a student puts forth a suggestion the teacher disagrees with, they don't come back with their own directive. Instead, the teacher reframes the suggestion, provides context for how the student might think about the problem differently, and gives the student ownership of coming up with a better suggestion. They use the illusion of choice to establish commitment—a tactic used in many negotiation scenarios.

Turning our attention back to our sales coaching example, suppose the rep suggested making forty prospecting calls, which the leader felt was too low. They could coach the rep to come up with a better suggestion by saying, "Based on the typical conversion rate we're seeing for prospecting calls, I'm not sure making forty of them will be enough to hit your goals. What do you think?" From there, the rep can reconsider their suggestion and come up with a more reasonable one to which they are committed.

Coaching Action Planner

As we explored in chapter 4, one of the most important sales leadership behaviors is driving mutual accountability between ourselves and our teams. And one of the most effective ways to do that is to write things down. This is especially true when it comes to coaching, so if you need a quick refresher, take a break to review that chapter again. But in addition to all of the tactics we covered earlier for documenting those critical conversations, there's an extremely helpful tool you can use to keep your coaching accountable and organized. I call it the Coaching Action Planner, and it's based on an approach I first learned from Mark Roberge, the founding VP of sales and former chief revenue officer at HubSpot.

Here's an easy-to-use template:

PERIOD/MONTH: _____

Rep Name	Focus	Reason	Action	Measurement

To begin with, indicate the period for which you are documenting your coaching actions. I recommend doing this for a calendar month, but you can make the timeframe more or less granular if you prefer. Next, complete the remaining fields using this framework:

REP NAME: The name of the team member you're coaching.

FOCUS: What's the one skill or behavior you're working with that rep on developing during the period?

Here's where the diagnostic coaching tactics we covered in this chapter come into play. For example, the area of focus might include things like these:

- Prospecting call count
- Price discounting
- Quality of discovery questions

REASON: Why was that focus selected?

This is where you provide evidence or justification for why the thing you've chosen to focus on will have the biggest impact on the rep's performance. But keep it simple. The Leading Indicators Coaching Formula and the insights and alignment gained from your coaching conversations will play an important role here. Based on the examples in the previous column, the reasons might look like these:

- Rep-generated sales pipeline is not sufficient to hit targets.

- Transaction counts are in line with the team average, but overall revenue is lower as a result of above-average price discounting.

- Discovery call conversion rate is too low. The cause: the rep identified they are asking too many surface-level questions, and they need to dive deeper to explore the root cause of their customers' issues.

ACTION: What specifically do we plan to do in order to improve the area of focus?

Here you outline the prescriptive action you've agreed on with your rep for moving the needle on the skills or behavior you identified. For example:

- Increase prospecting call count

- Reduce average price discount given

- Ask why the customer hasn't been able to solve the problem on their own

MEASUREMENT: How will we know if the rep improved in the area we chose to focus on?

This field should outline the metric or behavior to which you'll hold the rep accountable. For example:

- Average weekly prospecting calls: fifty-five (up from thirty)

- Average monthly transaction discount: 12 percent (down from 21 percent)

- On every discovery call, the rep needs to ask their customer why they have not been able to solve the problem on their own

Besides its obvious organizational advantages, using this tabular framework has two big benefits. First, it helps you identify trends and patterns within the needs of your team and the enablement needs you might look to deploy on a broader scale. For example, you might notice that half of your team is working on reducing the magnitude of price discounts they're offering to customers during the last quarter of the year. This could signal the need for some additional group training on establishing the value of your solution or negotiation tactics heading into the final stretch.

The second and less obvious benefit is using this framework to help you manage up! In our initial discussion on accountability, we outlined the pressures sales leaders face when it comes to showcasing their knowledge of their own organization at board, investor, and executive meetings. The Coaching Action Planner is an ideal artifact for sharing or summarizing in these forums. Not only does it illustrate the importance you place on coaching and the areas of improvement you've identified, but it can also inspire other leaders across your organization to do the same, elevating the profile of the company in the process.

When to Let Your Rep Go

Even with a robust approach for diagnosing issues with your team's performance and for coaching reps to success, one of the most common questions I get from sales leaders in my practice is, "How do I know when it's time to let the rep go?" After all, there are many instances when, despite our best efforts, coaching for the behaviors we're after isn't possible or is no longer practical. And since the revenue we provide is the lifeblood of our business, it's our responsibility to keep the sales machine running as efficiently as possible. In fact, a recent study found that 78 percent of high-performing sales organizations indicated that a poor performer will be terminated within a year, compared to 63 percent of average organizations and 52 percent of underperforming organizations.

Here is my simple, four-question framework for deciding when to let a rep go.

1   **DO WE KNOW WHAT'S HOLDING THE REP BACK?** Diagnosing and understanding the challenge the rep is experiencing is the first required step. After all, if you don't know why they're not performing, you owe it to them to find out before you take further action. Once you've isolated the largest contributing factor to the rep's lack of success, move on to the next question.

2   **IS THE MISSING PIECE SOMETHING YOU CAN TEACH THEM? AND CAN THEY LEARN IT?** Once you've identified which skill, competency, or behavioral characteristic the rep is missing, the question is, Can the missing piece be taught and learned through coaching? For example, many of the skills referenced in this book, such as product or industry knowledge, cold-calling techniques, or negotiation tactics, can be acquired through coaching. Other more deeply entrenched personality traits such as integrity, drive, respect, and honesty cannot be acquired in the same way. If the missing piece can be coached, move on to the next question. If it falls outside of this scope of what can be realistically coached, it might be time to let them go.

3 **DO WE HAVE ENOUGH TIME TO COACH THEM THROUGH IT?** Businesses and coaches both don't have an unlimited amount of time to help reps acquire the skills they need to be successful. For example, spending 80 percent of your coaching bandwidth on a single rep in a large team doesn't make sense. The pace of innovation in your business segment or industry may also require your organization to execute at a certain speed to maintain your market position. If you indeed have (or had) enough runway to administer the coaching regimen the rep requires, move on to the next question. If you don't, it might be time to let them go.

4 **ARE THEY LEARNING IT QUICKLY ENOUGH?** As with the last question, your bandwidth is precious and limited. Even with a clearly identified skill gap, a plan to coach the rep through it, and enough time to administer that plan, many factors either within or outside your control might conspire against the rep learning quickly enough. Regardless, if you find the rep isn't making enough progress in the area they need to, it might finally be time to let them go.

Five Keys to Sales Coaching

Summarizing the insights we've covered so far, there are five principles that govern top-tier sales coaching.

1 **CONSISTENT:** Whether it's in the gym, in the boardroom, on the field, or on the sales floor, in the battle for progress, consistency beats perfection, motivation, and execution every time. Regular coaching sessions are essential for building strong relationships between coaches and sales reps. A consistent cadence also helps establish a rhythm of ongoing support and feedback, which is critical for driving continuous performance improvement over time.

PLANNING QUESTION: What cadence of one-on-ones will you be committing to with your team?

2   **DEFENDED:** Sales coaching should be given a high priority in terms of time and resources. Leaders should be willing to defend scheduled coaching time and ensure that it is not overshadowed by other priorities. Of course, scheduling conflicts with things like vacation time, business travel, and critical customer meetings are bound to come up. In those instances, the coaching time or format should be changed but not canceled. By elevating the importance of coaching and making it a non-negotiable part of the sales rep experience, leaders reinforce its value with their team and ensure both the experience and the outcomes of it are taken seriously.

PLANNING QUESTION: How will you commit to defending your one-on-one with a rep if the time cannot be maintained? Will you move it to a different day or time? Extend the duration of your next one-on-one? Or perhaps trade the traditional office setting for an offsite breakfast, coffee, or neighborhood walk that can be more easily accommodated?

3   **ALIGNED:** Sales coaching should be closely aligned with the needs of the rep as well as the broader enablement strategy of the organization. This means that coaching sessions should focus on the specific skills and behaviors that have been determined to lead to sales success on both fronts. This also means that the focus and skills should be dynamic, changing as needed to ensure they remain high-impact and relevant. The more aligned the coaching strategy, the higher your win rates will be.

PLANNING QUESTION: What topics and skills should be covered in the coaching session? How might these things be similar to or different from what was covered in the past?

4   **PREDICTABLE**: Sales reps should know what to expect when they walk into a one-on-one with their leader. But that doesn't mean the experience should feel repetitive or routine. The agenda for the meeting should be sent out ahead of time, and the relevant data points should be reviewed prior to the session in order to maximize the time for analysis and discussion. But to maintain the aligned and dynamic nature of the sessions, the agenda itself can and should vary from time to time. For example, it's reasonable for sessions at the beginning of the quota period to include a discussion of the rep's pipeline and how to ensure they're set up for success in that period. As the end of the quota period draws near, it's reasonable for discussions to become increasingly focused on topics relevant to the final approach. Conversations about career, individual goal progression, and important personal issues can happen anytime.

PLANNING QUESTION: What should my team expect going into our one-on-ones? For example, what data? What questions? What format?

5   **ACCOUNTABLE**: As we discussed in chapter 4, mutual accountability is a critical ingredient for being a great leader. This goes double for your sales rep coaching. Both sales reps and leaders should have tasks and responsibilities that arise from their coaching interactions, and everyone should be held accountable for doing what they said they were going to do. This means documenting key insights, takeaways, and to-do's and ensuring they are revisited as needed at each session. By creating a culture of mutual accountability, sales leaders can ensure that goals and expectations are clear and that everyone is working together toward them.

PLANNING QUESTION: How will we document and measure progress and do what we said we were going to do?

Before we move on to the final skill, it's important to appreciate that coaching is a collaborative and comprehensive process in which sales leaders guide and support their reps to reach their full potential. It's done by helping team members diagnose operational and execution-related issues, asking thought-provoking questions, setting goals, and agreeing on the actions needed to achieve them. Here, the focus is on promoting long-term development by overcoming near-term obstacles and building a foundation of resilience.

But even with a solid foundation of coaching, sales leaders need to be mindful of two important things. The first is the need to understand how we're doing in the delivery of our leadership services and opportunities to improve at it. The second is how to provide our reps with the directive, performance-oriented insights and guidance they so often need from us in order to achieve the outcomes they're looking for. That's what we'll be exploring in the next chapter.

6

Getting and Giving Feedback

Perception Is Reality

I used to manage a rep named Adam. I liked Adam. As a sales professional, he was diligent, skilled, and good with customers. From a manager's perspective, he was coachable and a team player, and he managed to hit his quota most months. He also aspired to lead a team of his own one day. Adam was particularly vocal in team meetings, and his superpower was the ability to enthusiastically galvanize the team around his rallying cries. This was a positive quality when it came to getting the team fired up for things like prospecting blitzes, new product introductions, and customer events. However, it was decidedly negative when Adam periodically shared emotionally charged constructive criticism about things like the comp plan in a group setting. "I don't understand it!" he would complain. "Why would the company set the plan up like this?" Distracted and unproductive chatter among the team would begin to percolate as the mob became restless.

After one particularly inflammatory meeting outburst, I asked Adam for a few minutes to chat. I told him that I appreciated his passion and I always encourage questions and constructive conversation. But if he aspired to be a leader, he needed to be more aware of the tone and forum in which he chose to share his strong opinions. "I'd love to see you lead your own team one day," I said, "but leaders don't complain to their teams. If you want others to see you as a leader, you need to carry yourself differently. Your comments need to be more thoughtful and constructive. Not *destructive*. If you develop a reputation with the senior leaders as being a complainer, it's going to be very difficult for me to advocate to promote you."

Adam nodded. "I totally get it," he said. "You're right. This is definitely an area I want to focus on improving. Thank you for working on it with me. I promise to do better."

At this point, I want you to imagine two different scenarios unfolding.

In the first scenario, Adam and I meet every week for our one-on-one. We talk about lots of helpful things, but the topic of his outbursts in team meetings doesn't come up and he doesn't ask me for feedback about it. Three months pass. I don't recall any incidents happening over that time, but then again, it hasn't been top of mind. At the three-month mark, the company releases a new version of the comp plan, and in the very next team meeting, Adam unleashes another destructive rant. Before reading on, consider how you might react to his behavior in this scenario.

Now imagine a second scenario where Adam and I still meet each week after that initial conversation and have a productive one-on-one. But each time we meet, he asks for feedback on how he's doing on the destructive comment front. He says, "David, you know I'm trying to be more thoughtful and constructive about the commentary I share in team meetings. How did I do over the past week?" Each week when I think about his performance, I'm reminded that he hasn't made any destructive comments. He seems to be getting better! Three months pass. Then at the three-month mark, the company releases a new version of the comp plan, and in that very next team meeting, the same destructive comments appear. Consider how you might react to his behavior in this scenario.

Adam's behavior when it comes to making destructive comments is identical in both scenarios. One incident in three months. The only difference is the frequency of the feedback he asked for along the way. Scenario one involved zero requests for feedback. In scenario two, the requests were weekly. How was your opinion of his progress different in each scenario?

Having posed this same question to hundreds of sales leaders in my practice, their answers are remarkably consistent. In the first scenario, most leaders perceive Adam as having made no progress. He hasn't changed and is still making destructive comments. In the second, most leaders see his transgression as a minor slip-up, a small bump in the road on an otherwise steady track record of progress. The reality of the destructive comment is the same. The way in which it's perceived is totally different.

As it turns out, when it comes to your team's perception of how you're doing as a sales leader, there's some powerful research to back up this fascinating result.

The Impact of Feedback Frequency

Marshall Goldsmith has been recognized as one of the top ten business thinkers and the number one executive coach in the world. He's also the author or editor of forty-eight books, including three *New York Times* bestsellers. In 2004, Goldsmith and his research partner

Howard Morgan wanted to understand what types of developmental activities would have the greatest impact on the effectiveness of executives. So they conducted a study reviewing the leadership development programs at eight major corporations from different sectors, covering 11,480 leadership participants.

Each organization used a variety of approaches, including onsite coaching, offsite training, long-form sessions, short sessions, external coaches, and internal coaches, as well as traditional classroom-based training and ad hoc, on-the-job mentorship. But they didn't rely on the participant's own degree of satisfaction or happiness with the program to assess the outcome. Instead, they surveyed over 86,000 of their co-workers and key stakeholders to measure the leaders' perceived increase in effectiveness three to fifteen months after their programs began.

They found that regardless of industry, geography, and even the development methodology used, one singular variable was critical to influencing the perception of that leader's degree of improvement: the frequency of dialogue and follow-up maintained by the participant with their colleagues. The largest group of employees perceived that leaders who engaged in open conversations with their team members about areas for improvement and consistently maintained communication with them witnessed significant progress. In contrast, leaders who lacked ongoing dialogue with their colleagues were perceived by the largest group of employees to have demonstrated only marginal improvement, barely surpassing chance levels.

These findings held true regardless of whether the leader had an external coach, an internal coach, or no coach at all. And again, they also held true regardless of whether the participants attended a five-day or one-day training program or did not participate in any training program.

The key lesson here is that we don't change when our behaviors change. We change when our behaviors are perceived by others to have changed. That means if your goal is to not only improve but also have your team see you as an effective leader, you need to build the habit of asking for their feedback more frequently. The other benefit of frequent follow-up is that engaging in these behaviors can help you form more positive relationships with people and groups within your organization. And, as we saw in chapter 1, having positive relationships is the single most important factor for building that critical core foundation of trust.

In summary, get in the habit of engaging in feedback and follow-up conversations with your team more often and encourage them to do the same.

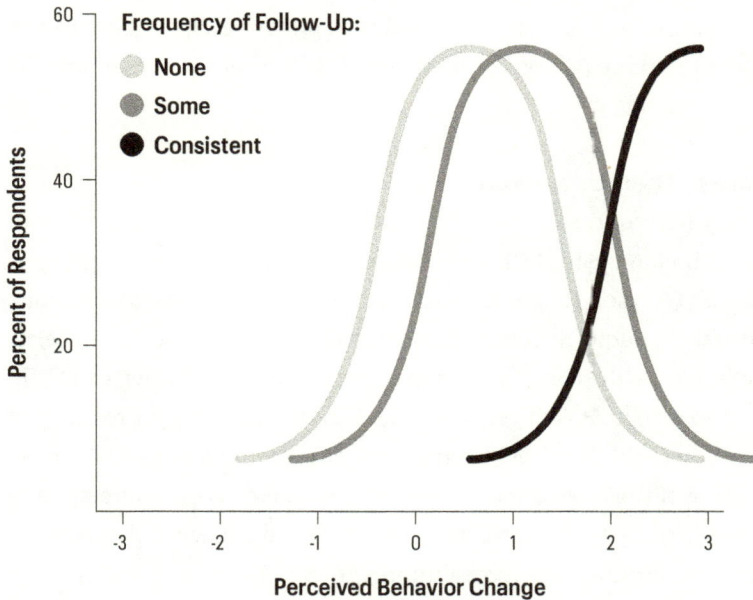

Source: Marshall Goldsmith and Howard Morgan, "Leadership Is a Contact Sport: The 'Follow-Up Factor' in Management Development," *Strategy + Business* 36 (2004): 76–77, marshallgoldsmith.com/wp-content/uploads/2022/05/LeaderContactSport.pdf. Used with permission.

How to Ask

Before we get into specific examples of exactly *what* to ask, it's important to address some of the key principles for *how* to ask for feedback in order to maximize the value of the experience.

Ask Often

The simple truth is, the more feedback you get, the faster you'll improve, both in reality and, as we've just seen, in the view of others. One of the other benefits of asking often is that it helps you overcome one of the biggest emotional barriers leaders have when it comes to feedback: the fear of what you might hear. After all, every time we ask others what they think about us, we put a little bit of our ego on the line. Like going to the gym, eating healthy foods, or going to bed on time, making asking for feedback a habit reduces the emotional barrier to doing it.

Address Their Unspoken Concerns

Getting helpful feedback from your team sounds easy enough, but the truth is, *they* might have fears and reservations about giving it. Deborah Grayson Riegel teaches leadership communication at Duke University's Fuqua School of Business and cites a number of concerns people have with giving their leaders feedback. Are you open to it? Will they "do it right"? Will getting critical feedback hurt your feelings or cause you to retaliate? Will you actually do anything with it? Addressing some of these issues preemptively can make people more open to the experience. Let your team know their feedback will help you keep your commitment to personal improvement. Assure them that while it might feel uncomfortable, you're very open to hearing anything they have to say. You can even preempt their feedback with your own thoughts on things you know you need to work on to get the ball rolling.

Flip the Focus

While getting constructive feedback about your personal leadership style is helpful, not everything can or should be about you. For example, you can ask for feedback about things like the quality or format of your team meetings, your team's relationships with other groups and departments at the company, and even policies and procedures. This will not only help instill feedback as a habit and create the perception of improvement but lower the emotional barrier for your team to respond as well. You'll be able to find examples later in this chapter.

Be Specific

One of the biggest barriers to getting helpful feedback is the perceived time investment on the part of the giver. That's one of the reasons why voluntary feedback surveys and website ratings are often polarized. In other words, people tend to volunteer feedback when they're absolutely delighted or extremely upset with the thing being asked about. One of the ways to encourage people to give helpful feedback is to reduce their time commitment by focusing the ask. For example, instead of asking "What do you think about...?" or "How do you suggest I...?" start your question with "What's one thing...?" Besides being easy to answer, simple, specific questions yield the most actionable insights.

Be Genuine

Have you ever seen an adult force a child to deliver an apology they didn't want to give? Chances are it lacked the authenticity that would make it seem sincere and believable. Unless you genuinely care about the feedback you're asking for, your team and colleagues can feel the same way. But being genuine in your desire for feedback isn't just about asking nicely. Feedback is a gift. So once you get it, be sure to thank the giver to show your appreciation. And more importantly, show people you've taken the feedback to heart by using it to make changes and improve. The approach we covered in chapter 3 on the advocacy feedback loop can be especially helpful here when it comes to sharing the impact of your team's feedback with them. The more seriously you take the feedback, the more likely others will be to give you more of it in the future.

Skip a Level

If you're a second- or third-level leader and above, make sure you create opportunities to get feedback from team members and leaders in your organization who don't directly report to you. Those skip-level coaching and feedback sessions are critical for three reasons. First, it shows your greater team that you're personally engaged and care about what they have to say, even though you may not always be as visible or present as their manager. Second, it helps you get feedback about your direct reports to help fuel your coaching conversations with them. And third, it helps you get critical and often hidden feedback that people may not feel comfortable sharing with their direct manager. As my parents would often say when my kids were little, "If we want to know what's going on in your house, we'll just take your kids out for ice cream and they'll tell us everything!" Don't underestimate the value of skip-level conversations when it comes to keeping your finger on the pulse of your team.

What to Ask

Combining all of the principles we've explored so far, here are some helpful categories and powerful questions to fuel your quest for feedback.

Personal Feedback

Here you're asking your team and colleagues for feedback to improve your personal performance and the things you can do to support theirs. For example:

- What's one thing I can do to better support you in your role?

- What's one thing I can do differently to support you and the team?

- What's one thing I can do to be a more effective manager/leader?

- What's one thing you'd like more feedback from me on?

- What's one key strength you think I should leverage more in my role?

- What's one thing I can do to help us be more effective in reaching our goals?

Operational Feedback

Here you're asking your team and colleagues for feedback to improve your operation from both tactical and strategic perspectives. For example:

- What's one thing we can do to improve how our team communicates?

- What's one thing that would make the revenue forecasting process easier?

- What's one key priority our team should be more focused on?

- What's one suggestion you have to improve our operation?

- What's one thing our executive team can do to better support us?

- What's the most important thing you feel our marketing team can do to support us?

Role Reversal

This simple approach asks the team member to put themselves in your position before answering the question. For example, you might ask your reps, "If you were me, what's one . . ."

- " . . . thing you'd do to help more people on our team hit their quota?"

- " . . . thing you would suggest I do to improve the quality of our team meetings?"

- " . . . thing you'd do to help our team perform at their best?"

- " . . . insight you feel it would be important to share with our executive team?"

- " . . . key initiative you'd ask our marketing team for more support on?"

Role-reversal questions are powerful for a number of reasons:

1 **HIDDEN INSIGHTS:** There are perspectives and opportunities for improvement that you, as a sales leader, simply won't see from where you sit. Granting your team hypothetical leadership power and authority creates a safe space for them to share insights you might otherwise miss or not appreciate. This is also one of the benefits of the deputizing exercise we discussed in chapter 4. Giving your team the freedom to flex their leadership muscles creates unique learning opportunities.

2 **EMPATHY:** It can be tempting for team members to play armchair quarterback and be critical of the decisions you make. Asking your team to consider questions and opportunities from your perspective shows them how complex your job can be and gives them an appreciation for the delicate balance leaders need to strike.

3 **COACHING OPPORTUNITY:** As we discussed in chapter 5 in the section about reframing reps' responses to coaching questions, not every suggestion our team members make is good. Some might require additional context, guidance, and consideration. Role-reversal situations present an ideal opportunity for this because our feedback can be framed as coaching. For example, suppose you asked, "If you were me, what's one thing you'd do to help more people on our team hit their quota?" To which the rep might respond, "I'd set lower quotas." You could invoke the power of transparency and coach the rep on how quotas are set by the finance team through a rigorous modeling process.

4 **HUMILITY:** Engaging in role-reversal dialogue sends your team the message that your judgment is not above reproach and that you welcome their perspectives and even their criticism if their approach might be different from yours. In fact, research has found that when teams observe altruistic behaviors like this from their managers, they are more innovative, make better suggestions for improving the way they work, and are more willing to go above and beyond the call of duty.

Survey Format

Free-form feedback questions can be very powerful in sales coaching conversations, allowing you to zero in on specific topics with great agility. But structured survey-based feedback can be equally helpful for a few reasons. First, surveys are objective and their results are easily quantifiable. Second, when administered periodically, surveys allow leaders to assess areas of growth and gauge progress over time. Third, surveys are time-efficient and allow multiple respondents to provide feedback over a consistent set of questions. This supports benchmarking against internal or external standards, enhancing the value of the results.

When I managed a large commercial sales team, we came up with a simple seven-question survey that ticked all these boxes and covered many of the key principles in this book. We've explored some of these already, and here's my latest version of them. You're welcome to borrow as many of them as you like!

1 **Providing great one-on-one coaching is one of the most valuable things sales leaders can do for their reps. How often does your manager meet with you one-on-one?**

On the surface, ensuring you're meeting with your reps frequently enough throughout the month is important when it comes to coaching. But the answer to this question is also helpful from an alignment perspective because leaders can sometimes overestimate the extent to which they're meeting with their reps. For example, you might consider the four-minute chat you had with your rep in the hallway on your way to your next meeting a one-on-one. Your rep may not share the same view. As a second-level leader or above, you can also use the answers to this question to help assess the extent to which your managers are coaching their teams consistently. If the number is on the lower end and you are focused on improving it, the survey results can help you gauge your managers' progress over time.

2 **On a scale of one to five, how helpful are those one-on-one coaching sessions?**

Value is in the eye of the beholder. While you might feel those one-on-ones were helpful, as before, it's important to ensure you and your team are aligned. As we saw in chapter 5, 82 percent of sales leaders believe they're providing their reps with coaching, but only 48 percent of salespeople report feeling like they are getting coached. If the answer to this question is a three or less, it's time to dig in and understand where the disconnect is and how you can improve the value of those meetings.

3 **Does your sales leader understand your strengths and areas for development, and do they work with you to grow your skills and career? (Yes/No)**

Research shows that the second-biggest reason employees become disengaged and leave companies, besides compensation, is because they lack career development opportunities. In fact, more than three-quarters of employees feel they don't get the help and guidance they need on the career front, leaving this important task completely up to them. This is especially true in sales because of the numerous directions a career in sales can lead. On the flip side, sales leaders who lean in and take a personal interest in guiding their reps' careers will find they've built team members for life.

4 **Do you know where you stand in terms of the progress toward your next role? (Yes/No)**

As the saying goes, if I had a nickel for every sales rep who felt they were ready to be promoted to the next stage of their career but weren't... Salespeople are ambitious and like the feeling of progress both on and off the dashboard. That's why one of the biggest challenges sales leaders face is managing the expectations of reps when it comes to career progression. To reduce the sense of distraction and uncertainty here, one of the best things leaders can do is develop a clear set of progression criteria. The story we explored in chapter 2 of how one chief revenue officer crafted an objective set of performance and learning metrics that provided certainty and transparency into this process for his reps is a perfect example of this.

5 **What is one thing your manager could do more of? And less of?**

As we explored in chapter 1, you probably already have a sense of the things you'd like to do more of and less of in your role. Now it's time to hear what your team thinks! While these focused "one-thing" questions are easy enough to rattle off during your one-on-ones, asking for feedback in survey format allows you to systematically capture these insights. The key here is not to focus on or elevate specific data points. Rather, identify trends and patterns. An example might be comments revealing an underlying sentiment of the reps wanting more personal attention or less micromanagement.

6 **Does your manager have your back? (Yes/No)**

In chapter 3 we explored the concept of advocacy and why, as Simon Sinek states, "good leaders make you feel safe." When sales leaders establish a circle of safety around their teams and look out for and defend them, they allow new levels of discretionary effort to be unlocked. This question speaks to the critical foundation of trust upon which the relationship with your team is built.

7 **Would I fight to work for my current manager again? (Yes/No)**

Here is where it all comes together! If you're doing most of the positive behaviors I've covered in this book consistently, seeing at least 80 percent of your team line up to work with you again should be easy to achieve. It also means you should be experiencing much of the upside in terms of team effort, retention, growth, and attainment. If you score less than that, it's important to dive deeper and understand where the issues might lie.

Giving Feedback

In her bestselling book *No Hard Feelings: The Secret Power of Embracing Emotions at Work*, co-author Liz Fosslien discusses some whimsical cookie-based analogies for how feedback can be given. These include the Oreo, two positive thoughts wrapped around a negative one (also known as the compliment sandwich or the shit sandwich); the oatmeal raisin, positive with bits of negative sprinkled in; and the sugar cookie, overly sweet and ultimately unfulfilling. But regardless of how you choose to deliver feedback to your team, if your goal is to genuinely help them improve, there's only one important thing you need to do. And I bet you already know what it is.

Think back to your childhood for a moment. Imagine you're heading out to school one morning, and as you sprint past the front door, the booming voice of a parent or guardian stops you dead in your tracks. "Hold on! Get back here!" they shout. After giving you a good look up and down, they continue, "You're not going to school looking like *that*, are you?" They then offer a passionate critique of your choice of clothing or hairstyle, or point out the food stain on the shirt you're sporting from the day before. After launching a short volley of futile objections, you relent and head back in to remedy your gross infraction.

Is the interaction irritating? Yes. Were the words spoken harsh and direct? Yes. But would you tolerate that type of "verbal abuse" from just anyone? Say, the barista at your local coffee shop, the driver of the bus that takes you to work, or the cashier at the supermarket checkout? Of course not! Then why did you allow it in these instances as a kid? Or better yet, why might you still tolerate the same type of pointed feedback from people like your spouse, partner, children, or best friend? The answer is simple: caring. When you truly care about someone and they know it, you've earned the right to challenge them directly.

Radical Candor

Kim Scott experienced this phenomenon personally. She had just joined Google and was giving a big presentation to the founders and the CEO about how their AdSense business was doing. She was expectedly nervous but was in the fortunate position of delivering good news. The business was firing on all cylinders, and when she presented the numbers, the CEO, Eric Schmidt, was blown away. He applauded her efforts and asked her what she needed to maintain the incredible momentum. By all measures, the meeting was a success.

Scott's boss at the time was Silicon Valley titan Sheryl Sandberg, who went on to become Meta's COO and board member. After the meeting, Sandberg suggested they debrief. She agreed that both the meeting and the team's success were very positive. Yet, Scott could sense some critical feedback marching in the direction of the conversation, which it did. "You said 'um' a lot," Sandberg shared. Scott didn't seem too frazzled. After all, she knew that was something she did, and it hadn't seemed to affect the outcome of the meeting.

Sandberg continued to question the "um"-filled narrative, asking if Scott's habit was fueled by nervousness, and even proposed having Google hire a speaking coach for her. Scott continued to minimize the feedback and instead focused on the success of the meeting. Finally, seeing as how her team member simply wasn't getting it, Sandberg decided to take a more direct approach. "You know, Kim," she said, "I can tell I'm not really getting through to you. I'm going to have to be clearer here. When you say 'um' every third word, it makes you sound stupid." Scott's focus instantaneously narrowed as the clarity of Sandberg's words finally sunk in. Years later, Scott coined a term that became the title of both her bestselling book and the company based on what she experienced that day: radical candor.

The idea is simple. The more you care about someone personally (not just the results they produce), the more you're able to challenge them directly about their behaviors and decisions. As Scott says, "Caring personally makes it much easier to do the next thing you have to do as a good boss, which is being willing to piss people off."

Ryan Barretto is the president of Sprout Social and presides over the revenue machine that helped scale the social media management platform from $30 million to over $300 million in annual recurring revenue during his tenure, securing an IPO along the way. He often shares a story with his team of how Sprout's CEO, Justyn Howard, gave him feedback after one of the key meetings in their IPO investor roadshow. As the meeting wrapped up, Howard asked Barretto to ride solo with him to the next meeting, with everyone else jumping in another car. During the ride, Howard pointed out some of the specific misses Barretto had related to the positioning of their company against their main competitor. The insights were real-time and direct and included specific examples of what Barretto had said in the meeting and suggestions to improve the impact of his narrative. "It was such an empowering moment for me," Barretto told me. "There was a lot of trust and respect in Justyn's feedback. I knew he believed in me and just felt my messaging needed a few tweaks. And for the rest of the IPO roadshow, I nailed it! But if he hadn't cared enough to share, I would have been hurting both my and the company's brand as we worked through the process."

Barretto believes that one of the keys to his company's incredible growth and success is fostering an environment where honest feedback is not only encouraged but also deeply rooted in their culture, as are many of the leadership principles we've covered so far in this book. Specifically:

PROTECTING AND ADVOCATING: If the goal is to create a culture where leaders and team members truly have each other's backs, it's not only helpful but a *responsibility* to give each other the feedback we need to improve. Barretto says that at Sprout they believe "feedback is having someone's back." But to make that possible, an environment of safety needs to exist for people to feel comfortable about being open and vulnerable. That safety needs to extend to even the most senior leaders as well.

TRANSPARENCY AND TRUST: The best sales leaders are clear about the winning behaviors their teams need to demonstrate to achieve the big goals they've set. They also care deeply about their people and take the commitment they've made to their growth and success seriously. It's this foundation that makes it possible to challenge people directly because they're clear on where the sentiment comes from.

PROMOTING ACCOUNTABILITY: To build the best sales teams, it's important to hire people who are on a journey of continuous self-improvement—those who know the best performances of their career lie ahead of them. Since they crave growth, feedback is a critical ingredient for holding them accountable to the commitment they've made to themselves.

The good news is, if you've been following all the approaches we've covered in this book so far, nailing this high-impact feedback formula should be easy! If you haven't, you may find yourself falling back into less-effective modes for delivering the feedback you need for your reps to perform at their best.

The Winning Feedback Formula

When you fall into the trap of softening critical feedback by incorporating praise because you're afraid of hurting someone's feelings, you diminish its value. If people have a strong self-image, critical feedback can be easily diluted by their ego. More sensitive team members can take the feedback much too personally. And without a roadmap to help them navigate what they're hearing, driving the behavioral change your feedback is meant to promote becomes very difficult.

Ironically, when we give people critical feedback, we often don't provide them with enough context to curb the undesirable behavior. For example, saying "Your sales forecasts are always way off" or "The discounts you're giving customers in your negotiations are much too high" doesn't help the person do better. The same thing happens on the positive side. For example, saying "Great job running that customer meeting! They were engaged the whole time" or "I love the way you handled that price objection!" may give the rep a temporary ego boost. But if you don't share enough insight for the person to know how to repeat the great thing they did, they might very well not.

But giving helpful, direct feedback is easier than you think. All you have to do is follow a simple three-step process.

STEP 1: IDENTIFY THE SPECIFIC BEHAVIOR. Whether it's something you'd like to see stopped, changed, or repeated, it's important to call out the behavior itself. This should be a clinical exercise, which means any emotional undertones should be left out. Just stick to the facts. For example:

INSTEAD OF SAYING: "The discounts you're giving your customers are insane!"
START WITH: "I noticed your average price discount is 32 percent, which is 13 percent higher than the team average."

INSTEAD OF SAYING: "I just can't trust your sales forecasts. You need to take off the happy ears!"
START WITH: "The data shows that 75 percent of your deals don't close when you initially forecasted them to."

INSTEAD OF SAYING: "Your prospecting emails are way too long, and the tone is much too aggressive."
START WITH: "I've noticed your prospecting email conversion rate is 5 percent compared to the team average of 15 percent."

INSTEAD OF SAYING: "The intro presentation you gave the customer was amazing!"

START WITH: "The agenda you put together for the customer presentation clearly highlighted their current issues and desired future state."

STEP 2: HIGHLIGHT THE IMPACT OF THE BEHAVIOR. Here's where you explain the implications or "so what?" behind the rep's actions. It's also a perfect example of how you can invoke the power of transparency we discussed in chapter 2. By providing the rep with the background, reasons, or rationale behind why you've decided to call out the behavior, you're closing the logic loop and creating certainty in their mind. After all, if you didn't feel the behavior was important, you wouldn't have called it out. For example:

> "Giving large discounts not only means it'll be harder to make your quota, but it also makes our solution seem less valuable in the minds of our customers."

> "The board uses sales forecast data to make key budgetary decisions that impact our department. If the forecast isn't accurate, it could come back to bite us."

> "Using those types of messages in your prospecting emails makes it hard to generate the pipeline you need, and if the tone is too aggressive, it could turn customers away from us for a long time."

> "At a time when customers choose vendors based on the experience they have with them, not just their solution, showing them you did your homework and came to the presentation prepared goes a long way to winning their business."

STEP 3: DISCUSS SPECIFICALLY WHAT THEY SHOULD DO MOVING FORWARD. In many ways, this step is a specific use case for the coaching approaches we discussed in chapter 5. That means you have two options here. First, you can be directive and tell the rep exactly what to do. Alternatively, you can engage the rep in a discovery-based discussion and ask them for suggestions on how they feel they should proceed. In either case, you should come to a mutual agreement as to how specifically the behavior will take shape moving forward. For example, your discussion may include directions and questions like these:

"Over the next thirty days, let's focus on not giving any discounts greater than 20 percent. Do you think that's reasonable?"

"What's one thing you can do over the next month that you believe would have a massive impact on the accuracy of your forecast?"

"I'd like you to craft a prospecting email that's at least 50 percent shorter than what you've been using and make sure you use an interest-based call-to-action instead of requesting the customer meet with you at a specific time."

"At our next team meeting, I'd love for you to give a five-minute overview of the steps you went through to prepare for that executive presentation, including any tools, sites, or templates you used. We can post everything to our learning hub to make sure everyone can replicate your winning formula. Are you up for that?"

As your feedback discussions unfold, it's critical to ensure you combine any instructions or follow-up behaviors you agree on with the rep with the approaches to driving coaching accountability we've explored so far. This includes things like writing down any relevant details in a mutually accessible location and letting your reports and dashboards do the hard work of monitoring progress, as discussed in chapter 4. And if the behavior is important enough to consume your near-term skill development focus, it might also mean updating your Coaching Action Planner, which we explored in chapter 5.

How to Have Hard Conversations

When it comes to giving feedback, most conversations are important, but not all of them are hard. The difference is that in hard conversations, the stakes are much higher, as is the potential emotional reaction of the sales rep. Conversations that end in the termination of the team member naturally fall into this category, but there are many others.

For example, one of my reps committed an offense that could have been fireable. They made a side agreement with a customer outside of our contract and had no idea it was against our rules. In another instance, I had a rep who acted inappropriately at a party. In both cases, when it came time for us to have a serious conversation behind closed doors, both reps were justifiably shaken and fearful. As a sales leader, if you want those hard conversations to produce the best results, it's even more important to approach them with the right mindset, words, and body language, and differently than your typical one-on-ones.

Mind Your Mirroring

Mirroring is a phenomenon in behavioral science that describes a situation where one person imitates the behavior, gesture, posture, attitude, or speech pattern of another person. When we observe others exhibiting the same behaviors as us, we feel connected to them, and rapport is more quickly established. Numerous studies prove this approach's powerful impact when it comes to influencing others. For example, in courtroom settings, legal teams that mirrored the judges' linguistic styles were statistically more likely to win their cases to a significant degree. In a 2002 study, Dutch researcher Rick van Baaren found that restaurant servers were able to increase their tips by 70 percent simply by repeating their customers' orders back to them exactly.

Mirroring can go beyond words and into body language as well. Researchers have praised the "chameleon effect," in which you imitate the movement and tone of the other person. Doing so can help bring a sense of safety and cohesion to a conversation. It's no surprise that salespeople are taught to use this approach in customer interactions and do it both on purpose and subconsciously. But when it comes to having hard conversations with your reps, mirroring can sometimes make things worse.

When a frightened, concerned, or angry employee walks in the door for a tough meeting, it's likely their body language will be closed off. As the book *Effective Difficult Conversations* by Catherine Soehner and Ann Darling explains, "we can let our body unconsciously mirror" behaviors such as crossed arms, a scowl, and a lack of eye contact, "or we can assert some discipline and hold an open body position, direct eye contact, and a slight smile." Leaders who are mindful of their posture are more likely to help lessen the anxiety and have a productive dialogue.

The same is true for language. If an employee says something out of anger or fear that isn't crucial to the conversation, echoing it won't help. But repeating key points while maintaining open body language helps a great deal. "You didn't know that was a rule." "You had too much to drink, and you feel terrible about it." "Challenges with some prospects were beyond your control." By saying these kinds of things, I could show my employees that I heard them and that, despite the circumstances, I still respected how terrible they felt. This can be especially helpful when these conversations take place by phone, without the benefit of eye contact and body language.

If an employee has misbehaved or broken a rule, you may wonder, why try to help them feel comfortable? Of course, being clear, confident, and direct is important. But in the examples I mentioned, working to calm things down and ensure we heard each other led to a positive outcome. The first rep was given a chance to express their remorse for breaking a rule, open up about how awful they felt, and take steps to rectify the mistake. They went on to be an even better employee. The salesperson who acted up at the party chose to resign and take steps to avoid repeating such behavior in the future. They understood that staying would have meant facing certain consequences and that their workplace relationships were damaged. They took responsibility, owned their decision, and moved forward.

And while being laid off is painful no matter what, those I had to let go over the years at least understood the rationale. We were also able to talk about their positive and highly transferable skills that could point them in the right direction for the next stages of their careers.

Nothing makes difficult conversations easy. And engaging in the positive uses of mirroring while avoiding the pitfalls can feel like a balancing act. But the more genuine your effort is to navigate these conversations, the more successful you'll be.

Closing the Loop on Feedback

Bringing our attention back to the key elements of getting and giving feedback, it's helpful to take a moment to step back and evaluate how you're doing in this area. Consider how you might moderate your feedback behaviors to add more value to both you and your team across these dimensions.

FREQUENCY: How often are you asking for feedback from your team today? How often would you like to ask (or should ask), moving forward? Are you asking often enough to show your team you're committed to learning and self-improvement? If you're a second- or third-level sales leader or higher, how often should you be asking for skip-level feedback so you can provide helpful coaching to your leadership reports and for the benefit of your overall operation?

AUDIENCE: Who do you typically solicit feedback from? Are your requests focused on your direct reports or your manager? Is there an opportunity to expand or shift the source of that feedback from time to time? For example, would it make sense to solicit feedback from your peers or other key departmental leaders across your organization on a regular but less frequent basis than your direct reports?

FORMAT: What modality are you using to source feedback today, and how might you see that changing moving forward? For example, do you see an opportunity to do more ongoing, standardized surveys? Or would you simply like to ask for more ad hoc feedback during the regular one-on-ones or team meetings you already have?

FOCUS: What topics are your requests for feedback centered on today? Are those the right ones? Are they helping you improve your operation and become a more effective sales leader? Are you focused on requesting personal feedback, operational feedback, or both? Do you have blind spots that require illumination?

QUESTIONS: What specific questions are you asking today? Are those the best ones to get the insights you're after? Are you shying away from asking tough questions for fear of what you might hear? How might you tweak your questions to solicit the helpful and actionable insights you're after? How would you moderate the type of questions you ask based on the audience and frequency?

DELIVERY: When it comes to giving feedback to your team and other key stakeholders, how are you doing with respect to identifying their specific behaviors and their impact on the business? Might you sometimes give general feedback that's hard to action, or are your insights direct and specific? Does your feedback have an emotional undertone that might undermine its reception by the other person? Does your feedback come from a place of genuine caring, and if so, does the receiver know and appreciate that?

Feedback is a fitting conclusion to our discussion of the five key skills sales leaders need to master because it embodies and reinforces so many of them. By asking for feedback, you create transparency about your desire for ongoing learning and the things you need to do in order to be a great leader. You foster an environment of safety and advocacy by showing your team that you're vulnerable and open to new perspectives and ways of doing things, as they should be. You demonstrate accountability to your team by showing them that you're putting the knowledge and insights they've shared with you to good use. And finally, feedback helps you make good on your commitment to coach your team and give them the insights they need to grow personally and professionally.

7

Your Sales Leadership Legacy

The Email That Changed Everything

"You around for a quick call to catch up?" This short email hit my inbox on July 17, 2008, at 2:32 PM. My stomach sank. It was from David Stein. It had been a few years since I had worked with him, but I knew what he had on his mind.

David was the co-founder of the startup I had joined as employee number twenty, and he was the very first sales leader I had worked under. He was super sharp and hard-working, and he had a high standard of performance, which I appreciated. He also practiced many of the skills we've covered in this book. Fate had caused our paths to first cross in early 2000 shortly after I was wrapping up my graduate work in engineering at the University of Toronto. It had been just a few weeks before I was supposed to start in a technical sales role at IBM that I was incredibly excited about, and he had told me he'd recently helped start a software company called Workbrain, something that was all the rage during the dot-com boom we found ourselves in the heart of. After hearing about my new job, he had suggested I come check out their office and meet the team. The experience of meeting those early team members, including their founder and CEO, David Ossip, was compelling, and I had decided to politely decline the IBM opportunity to join him on the adventure.

Over the next several years I learned a lot from David Stein as we fought side by side in the sales trenches, building Workbrain into a $100 million run rate business. After going through the turbulent acquisition I mentioned in chapter 2, David parted ways with the organization. Meanwhile, I stayed on and did my best to keep my crew together and help integrate our sales motion into the now much larger team. Nine months later, after a transformative eight-year run, things had stabilized, and I decided it was time for me to move on.

I was fortunate to be recruited by another high-growth startup that had a great team, significant funding, and a ton of momentum. It was the perfect opportunity to apply everything I had learned at my first venture to help make this one an equally great success. It also ticked a lot of the boxes I was looking for at that point in my career and life. The pay, commission plan, and equity grants were a generous upgrade, which was an important consideration for my growing family. I had the autonomy to build and lead a new team. I already had a number of friends there who had made a similar move from my first company. And shortly after I landed, I even brought some of my old team members over with me.

Several months into my new role, things were cranking! I was having an impact on the business, my wife and I had just welcomed our second daughter into the world, and the road ahead was full of promise. Life was good. Then I got that email from David.

Shortly after his departure from our first company, David had joined forces with Daniel Debow. Daniel was a friend, an original member of our first startup, and a fearless and formidable business strategist. They were catalyzing a new venture, a software company called Rypple. And precisely as I feared, my conversation with David ended in a request that I join them.

I was faced with an agonizing decision. On the one hand, I felt I had already made a commitment to my new company, their leadership team, and the people who had come over with me. I wasn't a quitter, and I wanted to see it through. Not to mention that leaving would mean giving up money, equity, momentum, and security for my family—all things I had worked so hard for. The gravity of my decision was further punctuated by the fact that, at the same time, the US economy was poised on the brink of collapse. If indeed I decided to make the switch and join them, I'd be starting from scratch. A brand new product, extremely limited resources, no sales or marketing motion, tons of risk. So I diplomatically declined.

But the conversation didn't end there.

David and Daniel were politely persistent, and our discussions continued in the days and weeks that followed. During that time I did a lot of soul searching. The way forward was no doubt uncertain and fraught with risk. But my drive to start something new and see what I was capable of with a leader from whom I had learned so much grew stronger. It's funny; when you hear the words "a sales leader you would fight to work with again," you don't often think about who or what you'd actually be fighting. In this case, the enemy was fear and incredible uncertainty. But my fight was apparently stronger. I made the decision to join Rypple. Three and a half years later, Rypple received an unexpected offer and was subsequently acquired by Salesforce in what was a terrific outcome for everyone. The trajectory of both my career and life changed forever, again. In total, David and I worked together for fourteen years across four companies, and we remain friends to this day.

A Sales Team for Life

It's clear that great sales leaders have a strong gravitational pull—one that can overcome many obstacles. As we discussed in chapter 1, they have hyper-engaged teams that take risks, push harder, don't want to let *them* down, and unleash the full force of their discretionary effort. The feelings of caring and personal and professional growth their reps experience are intoxicating. It's the reason that stories like mine aren't unique. Reps follow great sales leaders throughout their careers.

Unfortunately, sales leaders sometimes take a short-term view of their responsibilities. After all, in the hustle to hit your quota, you often find yourself deep in the weeds of your operation, whether it's helping orchestrate sales cycles, negotiating agreements, managing revenue expectations up the chain, or doing everything you can to squeeze every last dollar out of your pipeline as your deadlines loom. Tensions are often high on the sales floor. And as the number of solutions, technologies, and new categories of products explodes, the pressure to perform intensifies. It's no surprise that the average tenure of a VP of sales is on the decline, with some estimates putting it around seventeen months. But those who are intentional when it comes to leveraging the skills outlined in this book realize a surprising long-term benefit: they've built a sales team for life.

I've had a number of reps who've been on my team twice, and some even three times. To this day, I maintain wonderful relationships with so many of the people I've had the pleasure of leading over the years. Some of them have even gone on to become incredible sales directors, VPs, and CROs, leading teams of their own. I'm grateful that they still come to me for guidance. After all these years, every time I get a text from one of them that starts with "Hey Boss!" or "I could use some advice," or one of their reps gives them a shoutout on social media for how amazing they are, my heart lights up. The truth is, I still consider all of them to be part of my team and feel just as responsible for their growth and success as I did years ago.

In a profession so often plagued by poor experiences and bad reputations, great sales leaders are a beacon of light for their customers, companies, and teams. And their winning formula is simple: Be transparent with your people. Protect them. Make them feel safe. Hold them accountable for the things they need to do. Coach them to reach their full potential. Give them feedback to drive continuous improvement. And if you genuinely care about them and help them grow, you'll not only smash your revenue goals, but you'll also be a sales leader that changes the trajectory of their careers and their lives. The sales leader they need.

Notes

Chapter 1. Foundations of Great Sales Leadership

p. 6   *Eighty-three percent of organizations:* Laci Loew, "State of Leadership Development 2015: Time to Act Is Now," Brandon Hall Group, August 2015.

p. 7   *A recent leadership development study:* William C. Byham, "The Business Case for Leadership Development," Chief Learning Officer, August 17, 2017, chieflearningofficer.com/2017/08/17/business-case-leadership-development.

p. 11   *A recent study examined the brain processes:* Richard E. Boyatzis, Angela M. Passarelli, Katharine Koenig, Mark Lowe, Blessy Mathew, James K. Stoller, and Michael Phillips, "Examination of the Neural Substrates Activated in Memories of Experiences with Resonant and Dissonant Leaders," *Leadership Quarterly* 23, no. 2 (2012): 259–72, doi.org/10.1016/j.leaqua.2011.08.003.

p. 11   *Results from another study by researchers:* Jane E. Dutton, Kristina M. Workman, and Ashley E. Hardin, "Compassion at Work," *Annual Review of Organizational Psychology and Organizational Behavior* 1 (2014): 277–304, doi.org/10.1146/annurev-orgpsych-031413-091221.

p. 11   *In yet another study of 1,500 workers:* Jeanine Prime and Elizabeth Salib, "The Best Leaders Are Humble Leaders," *Harvard Business Review*, May 12, 2014, hbr.org/2014/05/the-best-leaders-are-humble-leaders.

p. 14   *The irony is that during the* COVID*-19 pandemic:* Morning Consult,
"The Future of Work: How the Pandemic Has Altered Expectations of
Remote Work," n.d., go.morningconsult.com/rs/850-TAA-511/images/
Remote%20Work%20Report%20-%20Morning%20Consult%20-
%20Final.pdf. This survey was conducted June 16-20, 2020, among a
nationally representative sample of 2,200 US adults.

p. 14   *In fact, data from the enterprise software firm Atlassian:* "People Are Working
Longer Hours during the Pandemic," *The Economist*, November 24, 2020,
economist.com/graphic-detail/2020/11/24/people-are-working-longer-
hours-during-the-pandemic.

p. 14   *For example, e-commerce giant Shopify outright banned:* Jena McGregor,
"This Company Is Canceling All Meetings with More Than Two Employees
to Free Up Workers' Time," *Forbes*, January 3, 2023, forbes.com/sites/
jenamcgregor/2023/01/03/shopify-is-canceling-all-meetings-with-more-
than-two-people-from-workers-calendars-and-urging-few-to-be-added-
back.

p. 15   *In fact, in her book* Radical Candor*:* Kim Scott, *Radical Candor: Be a Kick-Ass
Boss without Losing Your Humanity* (New York: St. Martin's Press, 2017), 25.

p. 15   *A 2019 study by Jack Zenger and Joseph Folkman:* Jack Zenger and Joseph
Folkman, "The 3 Elements of Trust," *Harvard Business Review*, February 5,
2019, hbr.org/2019/02/the-3-elements-of-trust.

p. 17   *Not surprisingly, out of 51,836 leaders studied:* Jack Zenger and Joseph
Folkman, "I'm the Boss! Why Should I Care if You Like Me?" *Harvard
Business Review*, May 2, 2013, hbr.org/2013/05/im-the-boss-why-should-
i-care.

p. 19   *In a sales effectiveness study:* Ryan Fuller, "3 Behaviors That Drive
Successful Salespeople," *Harvard Business Review*, August 20, 2014,
hbr.org/2014/08/3-behaviors-that-drive-successful-salespeople.

Chapter 2. Skill 1: Promoting Transparency

p. 31   *Sadly, according to Gallup's:* Ryan Pendell, "Employee Engagement
Strategies: Fixing the World's $8.8 Trillion Problem," Gallup Workplace,
updated September 11, 2023, gallup.com/workplace/393497/world-
trillion-workplace-problem.aspx.

p. 32   *The same organization conducted a meta-analysis:* Susan Sorenson,
"How Employee Engagement Drives Growth," Gallup Business Journal,
June 30, 2013, news.gallup.com/businessjournal/163130/employee-
engagement-drives-growth.aspx.

p. 32   *A different longitudinal study on employee engagement:* John Kotter, "Does Corporate Culture Drive Financial Performance?" *Forbes,* February 10, 2011, forbes.com/sites/johnkotter/2011/02/10/does-corporate-culture-drive-financial-performance.

p. 32   *Even a study of car rental sales reps:* Ahmed Khwaja and Nathan Yang, "Quantifying the Link between Employee Engagement, and Customer Satisfaction and Retention in the Car Rental Industry," *Quantitative Marketing and Economics* 20 (2022): 275–92, doi.org/10.1007/s11129-022-09253-6.

p. 33   *A study by McKinsey & Company:* Naina Dhingra, Andrew Samo, Bill Schaninger, and Matt Schrimper, "Help Your Employees Find Purpose— or Watch Them Leave," McKinsey Insights, April 5, 2021, mckinsey.com/ capabilities/people-and-organizational-performance/our-insights/ help-your-employees-find-purpose-or-watch-them-leave.

p. 33   *Millennials, who are forecasted to make up:* Alastair Mitchell, "The Rise of the Millennial Workforce," *Wired,* August 2013, wired.com/insights/2013/08/ the-rise-of-the-millennial-workforce.

p. 34   *Every month, as we close out our current month:* Mike Wolff, internal memo, August 2016. Used with permission.

Chapter 3. Skill 2: Protecting and Advocating

p. 51   *To earn it, heroes need:* US Department of Defense, "Description of Medals," Military Awards for Valor, n.d., valor.defense.gov/description-of-awards.

p. 51   *Since the Civil War, only 1,968 individuals:* US Department of Veterans Affairs, "Medal of Honor History," National Cemetery Administration, n.d., cem.va.gov/history/Medal_of_Honor_History.asp.

p. 52   *As the battle wore on:* Congressional Medal of Honor Society, "William D. Swenson," Stories of Sacrifice, n.d., cmohs.org/recipients/ william-d-swenson.

p. 52   *In his popular TED talk:* Simon Sinek, "Why Good Leaders Make You Feel Safe," TED talk, March 2014, ted.com/talks/simon_sinek_why_good_ leaders_make_you_feel_safe?language=en.

p. 53   *In his book* Leaders Eat Last: Simon Sinek, *Leaders Eat Last: Why Some Teams Pull Together and Others Don't* (New York: Portfolio/Penguin, 2017), 25.

p. 60   *In fact, a research study of nearly 300 leaders:* Andy Loignon and Stephanie Wormington, "Psychologically Safe for Some, but Not All? The Downsides of Assuming Shared Psychological Safety among Senior Leadership Teams," Center for Creative Leadership, 2022, doi.org/10.35613/ccl.2022.2048.

p. 62   *In it, authors Gary Keller and Jay Papasan introduce:* Gary Keller with Jay
         Papasan, *The One Thing: The Surprisingly Simple Truth behind Extraordinary
         Results* (Austin, TX: Bard Press, 2013), 106.

p. 66   *In fact, in a study conducted at Harvard University:* Diana I. Tamir and
         Jason P. Mitchell, "Disclosing Information about the Self Is Intrinsically
         Rewarding," *Proceedings of the National Academy of Sciences* 109, no. 21
         (May 2012): 8038–43, doi.org/10.1073/pnas.1202129109.

p. 69   *In Salesforce's 2018 State of Sales report:* Salesforce, *State of Sales*, 3rd
         edition, 2018, salesforce.com/form/conf/state-of-sales-3rd-edition.

p. 69   *In his popular TEDx talk:* William Ury, "The Power of Listening," TEDx talk,
         January 7, 2015, youtube.com/watch?v=saXfavo1Qo.

p. 72   *For example, in 2023, companies had their choice:* Scott Brinker, "2023
         Marketing Technology Landscape Supergraphic: 11,038 Solutions
         Searchable on Martechmap.com," ChiefMartec (blog), May 2, 2023,
         chiefmartec.com/2023/05/2023-marketing-technology-landscape-super-
         graphic-11038-solutions-searchable-on-martechmap-com.

Chapter 4. Skill 3: Driving Accountability

p. 85   *Former college president David Bednar told a story:* David A. Bednar,
         "Bear Up Their Burdens with Ease," Church of Jesus Christ of Latter-day
         Saints, April 2014, churchofjesuschrist.org/study/general-conference/
         2014/04/bear-up-their-burdens-with-ease.

p. 86   *"I was talking to a group of CEOs recently:* Dana Wilkie, "Your Employee
         Messes Up: How Do You Respond?" SHRM, August 29, 2017, shrm.org/
         resourcesandtools/hr-topics/employee-relations/pages/employee-
         mistakes.aspx.

p. 87   *For example, a study published in the* Journal of Occupational Health
         Psychology: Caitlin A. Demsky, Charlotte Fritz, Leslie B. Hammer, and
         Anne E. Black, "Workplace Incivility and Employee Sleep: The Role of
         Rumination and Recovery Experiences," *Journal of Occupational Health
         Psychology* 24, no. 2 (2019): 228–40, dx.doi.org/10.1037/ocp0000116.

p. 87   *A study published in the* Journal of Business Ethics: Clive R. Boddy,
         "Corporate Psychopaths, Conflict, Employee Affective Well-Being,
         and Counterproductive Work Behaviour," *Journal of Business Ethics* 121
         (2014): 107–21, doi.org/10.1007/s10551-013-1688-0.

p. 87   *And a study published in the* Academy of Management Journal: Bennett J.
         Tepper, "Consequences of Abusive Supervision," *Academy of Management
         Journal* 43, no. 2 (2017): 30, jstor.org/stable/1556375.

p. 88   *David Allen, management consultant:* David Allen, "About," Getting Things
Done, n.d., gettingthingsdone.com/about.

p. 93   *In fact, a study that analyzed:* Meg Prater, "How to Make the Best Follow-
Up Sales Call in 2021," HubSpot (blog), updated June 10, 2021,
blog.hubspot.com/sales/best-times-to-connect-with-leads-infographic.

p. 98   *In 2020, that number skyrocketed:* National Center Chronic Disease Prevention and Health Promotion, "Adult Obesity Facts," Centers for Disease
Control and Prevention, May 17, 2022, cdc.gov/obesity/data/adult.html.

p. 98   *In it, they ask, "Did you ever wonder why:* Jeffrey Pfeffer and Robert I. Sutton,
The Knowing-Doing Gap: How Smart Companies Turn Knowledge into Action
(Boston: Harvard Business School Press, 2000), 4.

Chapter 5. Skill 4: Coaching Your Team

p. 113   *Sales coaching and mentoring:* "Top-Performing Organizations Prioritize
Sales Enablement, Says Forbes Insights/Brainshark Report,"
Forbes, October 20, 2015, forbes.com/sites/forbespr/2015/10/20/
top-performing-organizations-prioritize-sales-enablement-says-forbes-
insightsbrainshark-report/#2f87c16c495d.

p. 113   *In a 2021 survey:* "2021 Sales Coaching Survey Results," Second Nature,
n.d., secondnature.ai/resources/sales-coaching-survey-2.

p. 113   *Of top-performing sales reps:* Jonathan Frick, Brian Gaffey, and Greg
Callahan, "Would Your Sales Reps Pay for an Hour of Their Manager's
Time?" Bain & Company, November 5, 2020, bain.com/insights/would-
your-sales-reps-pay-for-an-hour-of-their-managers-time-infographic.

p. 113   *Sales reps with at least two hours:* Jim Dickie and Tim Braman, "The ROI
of Great Sales Coaching," Revegy, May 15, 2015, slideshare.net/revegy/
the-roi-of-great-sales-coaching.

p. 114   *Companies with tailored sales coaching programs:* CSO Insights, *Fifth Annual
Sales Enablement Study*, Miller Heiman Group, 2019, salesenablement.pro/
assets/2019/10/CSO-Insights-5th-Annual-Sales-Enablement-Study.pdf.

p. 114   *Companies that provide quality coaching:* Robert J. Kelly and Greg Thomas,
Research Report: Supporting Sales Coaching, Sales Management Association,
November 2015, salesmanagement.org/web/uploads/pdf-renamed-by-
uzzal/89f5f8ff556f7a60adf7f1a78eac94c1.pdf.

p. 114   *According to a survey conducted by* Harvard Business Review: "How to
Predict Turnover on Your Sales Team," *Harvard Business Review*,
July–August 2017, hbr.org/2017/07/how-to-predict-turnover-on-your-
sales-team.

p. 114   *And Salesforce's 2022 State of Sales report:* Salesforce, *State of Sales*, 5th edition, 2022, salesforce.com/content/dam/web/en_gb/www/pdf/state-of-sales-5th-edition.pdf.

p. 114   *But in a world where 96 percent of employees say:* Jack Zenger and Joe Folkman, *How Developing a Coaching Culture Pays Off*, Zenger Folkman, 2019, zengerfolkman.com/wp-content/uploads/2019/08/How-Developing-a-Coaching-Culture_WP-2019.pdf.

p. 114   *A study by the Sales Management Association:* Kelly and Thomas, *Research Report*.

p. 115   *It's not surprising, then:* Jim Keenan, "Salespeople Who Exceed Quota Are 32% More Likely to Be Coached," *Forbes*, August 7, 2018, forbes.com/sites/jimkeenan/2018/08/07/salespeople-who-exceed-quota-are-32-more-likely-to-be-coached/?sh=abc3e551f57c.

p. 115   *Research from Bain & Company showed:* Frick, Gaffey, and Callahan, "Would Your Sales Reps Pay for an Hour of Their Manager's Time?"

p. 116   *She states that leaders often give this lament:* Maura Thomas, "To Control Your Life, Control What You Pay Attention To," *Harvard Business Review*, March 15, 2018, hbr.org/2018/03/to-control-your-life-control-what-you-pay-attention-to.

p. 116   *Finally, you find yourself in the same position as:* Tyler Spraul, "What Percentage of Gym Memberships Go Unused?" Exercise.com, updated November 30, 2023, exercise.com/learn/unused-gym-memberships-percentage.

p. 117   *A large-scale study of 2,000 global leaders:* Jack Zenger and Joseph Folkman, "Most Managers Think of Themselves as Coaches," *Harvard Business Review*, July 25, 2014, hbr.org/2014/07/most-managers-think-of-themselves-as-coaches.

p. 137   *Canadian professional tennis player Bianca Andreescu:* Myles Dichter, "Bianca Andreescu Prepared on All Fronts for Grass Season in Search of First Wimbledon Win," CBC.ca, June 12, 2022, cbc.ca/sports/tennis/tennis-bianca-andreescu-grass-season-1.6482781.

p. 137   *In a televised interview:* CBC News, "Bianca Andreescu Reflects on Taking Mental Break, Writing Children's Book," April 18, 2022, youtube.com/watch?v=RQpkhmfCubI.

p. 143   *In 1997, the* New York Times *published:* William Grimes, "In War against No-Shows, Restaurants Get Tougher," *New York Times*, October 15, 1997, nytimes.com/1997/10/15/dining/in-war-against-no-shows-restaurants-get-tougher.html.

p. 150   *In fact, a recent study found that:* Steve W. Martin, "What Top Sales Teams Have in Common, in 5 Charts," *Harvard Business Review*, January 20, 2015, hbr.org/2015/01/what-top-sales-teams-have-in-common-in-5-charts.

Chapter 6. Skill 5: Getting and Giving Feedback

p. 159   *Marshall Goldsmith has been recognized:* "Thinkers50 Hall of Fame 2018," Thinkers50, n.d., thinkers50.com/hall-of-fame/year-2018; "Meet Marshall," Marshall Goldsmith (website), n.d., marshallgoldsmith.com/meet-marshall.

p. 160   *So they conducted a study:* Marshall Goldsmith and Howard Morgan "Leadership Is a Contact Sport: The 'Follow-Up Factor' in Management Development," *Strategy + Business* 36 (2004): 71–79, marshallgoldsmith.com/wp-content/uploads/2022/05/LeaderContactSport.pdf.

p. 162   *Deborah Grayson Riegel teaches leadership communication:* Deborah Grayson Riegel, "How to Encourage Your Team to Give You Honest Feedback," *Harvard Business Review*, October 28, 2022, hbr.org/2022/10/how-to-encourage-your-team-to-give-you-honest-feedback.

p. 167   *In fact, research has found:* Jeanine Prime and Elizabeth R. Salib, *Inclusive Leadership: The View from Six Countries (Report)*, Catalyst, May 7, 2014, catalyst.org/research/inclusive-leadership-the-view-from-six-countries.

p. 169   *Research shows that the second-biggest reason employees:* PR Newswire, "How to Get Today's Employees to Stay and Engage? Develop Their Careers," June 3, 2019, prnewswire.com/news-releases/how-to-get-todays-employees-to-stay-and-engage-develop-their-careers-300860067.html.

p. 171   *In her bestselling book* No Hard Feelings: Kim Scott, Liz Fosslien, and Mollie West Duffy, "How Leaders Can Get the Feedback They Need to Grow," *Harvard Business Review*, March 10, 2023, hbr.org/2023/03/how-leaders-can-get-the-feedback-they-need-to-grow.

p. 173   *As Scott says:* "Radical Candor—The Surprising Secret to Being a Good Boss," The Review, n.d., review.firstround.com/radical-candor-the-surprising-secret-to-being-a-good-boss.

p. 179   *For example, in courtroom settings:* Maxim Sytch and Yong H. Kim, "Want to Win Someone Over? Talk Like They Do," *Harvard Business Review*, December 8, 2020, hbr.org/2020/12/want-to-win-someone-over-talk-like-they-do.

p. 179   *In a 2002 study:* Rick B. van Baaren, "The Parrot Effect: How to Increase Tip Size," *Cornell Hospitality Quarterly* 46, no. 1 (2005), doi.org/10.1177/0010880404270062.

p. 179   *Mirroring can go beyond words:* Kevin Ochsner, "Support Your Team... Quietly," *Harvard Business Review*, November 22, 2012, hbr.org/2012/11/helping-people-deal-with-emoti.

p. 179   *As the book* Effective Difficult Conversations*:* Catherine Soehner and Ann Darling, *Effective Difficult Conversations: A Step-by-Step Guide* (Chicago, IL: American Library Association, 2017), 51–52.

Chapter 7. Your Sales Leadership Legacy

p. 188   *It's no surprise that the average tenure of a VP of sales:* "Sales Vice President Demographics and Statistics in the US," Zippia, n.d., zippia.com/sales-vice-president-jobs/demographics; Hamish Knox, "Winning the War on the 17-Month Average Tenure of a VP Sales with Callan Harrington from Flashgrowth," *Full Funnel Freedom* (podcast), February 19, 2023, fullfunnelfreedom.com/podcast/winning-the-war-on-the-17-month-average-tenure-of-a-vp-sales-with-callan-harrington-from-flashgrowth; Jordan Wan, "30-60-90 Day Plan for a New VP of Sales," CloserIQ (blog), November 2016, closeriq.com/blog/2016/11/new-vp-of-sales.

About the Author

IKE MOST OF US, David Priemer never thought he'd end up in sales. He started his career tinkering with test tubes and differential equations as an award-winning research scientist before spending almost twenty years leading top-performing sales teams at high-growth technology companies, including Salesforce, where he was vice president of commercial sales and creator of the Sales Leadership Academy program.

Today, as the founder and chief sales scientist of Cerebral Selling, David is widely recognized as a thought leader in the areas of sales and sales leadership and is a sought-after trainer, leadership coach, and keynote speaker. Often referred to as the "Sales Professor," David is the author of the bestselling book *Sell the Way You Buy*, and his unique science- and empathy-based approaches to driving revenue and talent growth have been published in the *Harvard Business Review* and in *Forbes*, *Entrepreneur*, and *Inc.* magazines.

David holds a BSc in chemistry and atmospheric science from York University and a master's degree in chemical engineering from the University of Toronto. He blogs at cerebralselling.com.